Women, Men, and the Trinity

Women, Men, and the Trinity

What Does It Mean to Be Equal?

Nancy Hedberg

WIPF & STOCK · Eugene, Oregon

WOMEN, MEN, AND THE TRINITY
What Does It Mean to Be Equal?

Wipf & Stock
An Imprint of Wipf and Stock Publishers
199 W. 8th Ave., Suite 3
Eugene, OR 97401
www.wipfandstock.com

ISBN 13: 978-1-60899-199-0

Manufactured in the U.S.A.

*To my husband, LeRoy, a man of God
who has loved and encouraged me
all along the way.*

Contents

Introduction: What Is the Problem?

IF *I weren't a Christian, and I weren't a girl, I would do something with my life.* That was my coming-of-age self-talk regarding my future. Obviously I misunderstood what it means to be a Christ-follower as well as what it means to be a woman. It didn't take me long to understand that I was more likely to do something meaningful with my life as a Christian than as a non-Christian. However, I have spent a good part of my adult life unraveling my wrong thinking in regard to being a woman. How did God intend men and women to relate to one another? Did he mean the relationship to be hierarchical or egalitarian?

For many years I put the whole issue of woman's role on the shelf. I couldn't figure out whether God had intended a harmonious hierarchy with women cheerfully accepting their subordinate position as helper and childbearer or if he had intended an egalitarian community with women working alongside men in order to be fruitful and rule over creation. I just didn't know. But the scripture that helped me put the issue to rest for many years was Philippians 2:5–7: "Your attitude should be the same as that of Christ Jesus: Who, being in very nature God, did not consider equality with God something to be grasped, but made himself nothing, taking the very nature of a servant, being made in human likeness." This clearly states that our attitude is to be like Jesus' attitude. Jesus did not grasp for equality. Therefore, I decided that if women were equal to men, and God intended an egalitarian relationship between men and women, the Christlike attitude was to not grasp for that equality, but to be humble and submissive.

And for sure, if God intended men to be in authority over women, women shouldn't grasp for an equality that didn't exist. I couldn't decide whether God had intended a hierarchical or egalitarian relationship, but either way, I was confronted with Paul's admonition to have a Christlike attitude. Christ's attitude was one of humility, servanthood, and obedience.

THE PROBLEM

Adopting an attitude—the right attitude—is one thing. And it is a good thing. But it intrigues me that although several decades have passed since I first pondered the role of women, many of the same questions are calling for answers. I am still convinced that women should not grasp for equality—just as men should not grasp for superiority—but there are issues of truth, justice, and sensitive biblical interpretation that call for further exploration. Although scripture is clear about what our *attitude* should be, contemporary theologians hotly debate what the *reality* is. Are women equal to men? Today almost everyone would answer, yes, of course. But there's a catch. Many evangelical Christians insist that men and women are equal in *essence*, but that in *function* women are subordinate. We are equal in who we are, but not in what we do. This debate extends beyond the relationship between men and women. When Paul says, "the head of the woman is man, and the head of Christ is God" (1 Cor 11:3), he draws a parallel between the relationship of men and women and the relationship of the Father and Son within the Trinity. Today there are a number of conservative evangelical theologians who claim that although the Son is eternally equal to the Father in essence, he is eternally subordinate in function. I have always viewed the Father, Son, and Holy Spirit as equal within the Godhead and I find it difficult to understand how the Son can be both equal and permanently subordinate.

The purpose of this book is to explore equality within the Trinity and to see how Trinitarian theology might impact the relationship between men and women. I will make the case that equality of essence on the one hand, and permanent subordination in function on the other—whether applied to the Trinity or to the relationship between men and women—is a questionable premise and difficult to support logically, historically, or biblically. I will examine the historical, biblical, and current theological basis for this theory and evaluate its validity.

QUESTIONS WE MUST ASK OURSELVES

There are a number of questions calling for answers. For instance, what *about* the Trinity? Does the Bible teach that God the Son is equal to God the Father in both essence and function, or only in essence? What about the historic orthodox Christian view? Has the Church taught that the Son is eternally equal to the Father in both essence and function? Obviously the Son was subordinate to the Father during the incarnation, but is he eternally subordinate as well? In what ways can the relationship between men and women be compared to the relationship between God the Father and God the Son (1 Cor 11:3)? What was Paul's purpose in making that comparison? Another question has to do with Paul's use of the term *head*. Is he referring to hierarchical authority or to some other aspect of relationship? And finally, how has sin distorted the male/female relationship and how can it be restored?

THE WORDS WE USE

The words we use, and the fact that some people use them differently than others, can cause confusion and unnecessary misunderstandings. In the heat of debate it is tempting to take words out of context and use them against our opponents. In political campaigns we see this skill honed to perfection. But within the Christian community our goal should not be so much to win the argument as to come to a place of understanding. Even if we are unable to come to agreement, we should sincerely try to comprehend what the other person is saying and acknowledge the possibility of learning something from his or her perspective.

In order to foster as much understanding as possible, I want to explain some of the terms I will be using in this book. Two words I will use frequently are *role* and *function*. I will use them interchangeably. A function is a responsibility or office assumed by an individual. It refers to works or actions. Similarly, role refers to a part played or a position assumed for a specific period of time. Both words refer to actions or things people do. In contrast to function and role, I will also refer to *essence*. Essence means one's basic makeup, the essential traits retained as long as an individual exists—one's very nature. Questions regarding *functional* and *essential* equality are at the core of the current theological debate regarding the role of women.

Two other terms I will use frequently are egalitarian and complementarian, terms commonly used to indicate opposing views regarding the role of women. I will use the term complementarian to describe those who believe that women are equal to men in essence, but subordinate in function, and the term egalitarian to indicate those who believe that women are equal to men in both essence and function. In reality, both complementarians and egalitarians believe that, while different, men and women are complementary to one another. In that respect, it would be more accurate to refer to hierarchical-complementarians and egalitarian-complementarians. However, those are awkward terms and I will simply refer to complementarians and egalitarians with the understanding that when it comes to practical matters, the complementarian perspective is basically hierarchical. In a hierarchical system, persons are ranked from highest to lowest or assigned unchanging positions.

While complementarians discern a hierarchical ranking within the Trinity and in the relationship between men and women, egalitarians see equality and mutuality. Equality does not mean sameness. There can be equality and still be differences and orderings of one sort or another. To describe people or things as different from one another does not necessarily mean that one is better or higher. *Difference* merely indicates otherness. At the same time, *order* indicates relationship. While people or things can be ordered in relationship to one another, it does not mean that the ordering must be hierarchical.

When it comes to the Trinity, there is another important distinction that must be made—the distinction between *eternal subordination* and *incarnational subordination*. I think it is fair to say that all Christians recognize incarnational subordination, the submission of the Son to the Father during Jesus' incarnation. There are numerous biblical passages in which Jesus expresses his dependence upon his heavenly father and acknowledges his father's authority. But a number of current theologians argue for eternal subordination, the permanent functional subordination of the Son to the Father before, during, and after the incarnation. While not all complementarians believe in the eternal functional subordination of the Son, for many it is at the heart of their argument and central to today's theological debate.

The importance of understanding the different ways in which people use words is especially relevant in two chapters of this book. One is the next chapter, describing the current debate among evangelical theologians. If we do not understand what various theologians mean when they refer to things like functional subordination or essential equality, it will be difficult to follow their arguments. The other chapter in which the definition of terms is important is the chapter on the church's historical view of the Trinity. The focus of a debate can be different in one century than in another. For instance, the current debate about the Trinity focuses on whether the Father and the Son are equal in both essence and function or just in essence. In the fourth century, when the doctrine of the Trinity was being codified, the major concern was defending the deity of the Son. It is tempting to try to find in the words of the Church Fathers the answer to a question that wasn't being asked. The words, thoughts, and assumptions of early theologians are weighty and worth exploring. But they are not always easy to understand. The fact that learned and thoughtful current theologians—both egalitarians and complementarians—strongly disagree with one another while claiming that the orthodox Christian tradition supports their point of view, is an indication of the difficulty of discerning what early theologians were trying to say as well as how easily words can be twisted and misconstrued.

THEOLOGICAL ASSUMPTIONS

Although we all approach life with certain assumptions, we are not always aware of what those assumptions are until we run into something that challenges them. That was the case in the late 1970s when I read George Knight's book, *The New Testament Teaching on the Role Relationship of Men and Women,* and came across his claim that within the Trinity the Son is functionally subordinate to the Father. I had been taught—and still believe—that the Father and the Son were equal. Period. Knight's viewpoint challenged that assumption and planted a question in my mind. For the most part, I put the question aside for many years. Then I read Kevin Giles's book, *The Trinity and Subordinationism.* To a great extent this book is my attempt to come to terms with the opposing viewpoints of complementarians such as Knight, and egalitarians such as Giles.

The doctrine of the Trinity is one of the core distinctives of the Christian faith—some would say *the* core distinction of Christianity. Although it is impossible to completely grasp, it is important and worthy of exploration. In addition to identifying the God we worship, the doctrine of the Trinity impacts our understanding of relationships, community, and equality. Likewise, I believe the relationship between men and women is important to explore. Gender is the most basic of identifiers. "Is it a boy or a girl?" we ask when a child is born. On nearly every form we fill out we check a tiny box to indicate if we are male or female. As we enter adulthood, many of us give serious attention to finding a person of the opposite sex with whom we are willing to spend the rest of our lives. And so, it is important to explore the male/female relationship. How are we to understand these beings who are so different than we are? What works? What doesn't? And most important of all, what did God have in mind when he created us male and female, when he created us in such a way that the very continuation of the human race required male and female to come together in intimacy and interdependency?

Our primary source for understanding the nature of God and for getting his perspective on the makeup of men and women is the Bible. Although less important than the Bible, there are other things we must take into consideration. Historic orthodox Christian views, as well as current cultural realities must be considered when evaluating theological trends. Church history is made up saints and sinners, obedience and disobedience, heresy and orthodoxy. Likewise, our current culture, with its technological advances and scientific discoveries is both beneficial and detrimental to our understanding of reality. The secular bent of the world in which we live sometimes creeps into the church impacting our willingness to trust God and follow him in obedience. But when sanctified by the Holy Spirit, the Church, culture, technology, and science can lead us to a deeper understanding of God, his revelation, and his ultimate purposes. That is why, in this book I will be exploring all of these—the Bible, church history, and current theological and cultural trends.

The issues discussed in this book have practical implications regarding women in ministry. However, the major focus is not on questions of whether or not it is permissible for women to teach men or if women should be allowed to hold specific leadership positions in the church. Instead, the focus is on the philosophical and theological assumptions behind those questions and the attitudes with which men and women are called to relate to one another.

IS IT REALLY IMPORTANT?

There is a gridlock in many churches today regarding the role of women. It is also an issue at Christian colleges and seminaries. Training women for ministry, on the one hand, while at the same time warning them they must limit their ministry to positions that are *OK* for them, creates confusion and disillusionment. When I am in a group of Christians who take the equality of women for granted, I ask myself what the fuss is all about. Why am I spending so much energy exploring the role of women and issues of equality when it seems to be a non-issue? But the next day I might be in another group of Christians who look at things differently. Then I remember. One time I was helping at a parachurch function. At the last minute the organizer asked me to pull together some people to take the offering. I found some men and women who were willing to help and jotted their names on a slip of paper. When I handed the list to the event organizer he seemed embarrassed. "Umm," he said, "I don't think we can have women taking the offering." I was stunned. It hadn't occurred to me that helping take an offering might be considered an inappropriate way for women to serve. At times such as that I know that the role of women is still an issue!

2

Theologians: What Are They Thinking?

A s I mentioned in the previous chapter, there is a gridlock in many churches today regarding the role of women. In this chapter we will explore several points of disagreement between egalitarians and complementarians, paying special attention to the argument that it is possible to be equal in essence and at the same time permanently subordinate in function. Because much of this debate is focused on the "headship" Paul mentions (1 Cor 11:3), and because in that same passage Paul refers to the order of creation, we will start by comparing how complementarians and egalitarians interpret the creation narrative in Genesis. After that we will look at the arguments for and against permanent functional subordination. In the final section of this chapter we will see how current theologians believe the concept of functional subordination impacts issues of authority and submission, both within the Trinity and between men and women.

CREATION ORDER

It is common for both complementarians and egalitarians to refer back to the creation narrative as a basis for their respective views on women. Many complementarians believe that one of the reasons men have authority over women is because God created man before woman and woman was created for man. For instance, referring to Paul's comments in 1 Corinthians 11:8 regarding head coverings and in 1 Timothy 2:13 regarding women being silent in the church, Bruce Ware concludes that the order of creation signifies men's authority over women. "Further, in 1 Corinthians 11:9 Paul indicates that the man was not created for the woman's sake but rather the woman was created for the man's sake, and because of this, women should recognize male authority in the Christian community."[1]

In addition to the order of creation argument, some believe the fact that Adam named Eve, has significant implications. "When Adam named her—a prerogative in the Old Testament of one having authority—he demonstrated his authority over her."[2] Complementarians see this authority issue impacting such things as whether or not women should instruct men, teach doctrine, or exercise spiritual authority.[3] When discussing whether or not women should be allowed to teach men, Wayne House explains that Paul's prohibition has a theological basis—"the priority of man in creation and the deception of Eve in the fall."[4]

It is this argument regarding God's creative order to which complementarians return again and again. Upon what does Paul base his regulations regarding marriage? "Paul . . . shows that his regulations for marriage also flow from this *order of creation*."[5] Why did Satan approach Eve rather than Adam? "Satan's subtlety is that he knew the *created order* God had ordained for the good of the family, and he deliberately defied it by ignoring the man and taking up his dealings with the woman."[6] Why are men and women assigned different ministry roles? "The differentiation of roles for men and women in ministry is rooted not in any supposed incompetence, but in God's *created order* for manhood and womanhood."[7] Why should the patriarchal system not be consid-

---

1. Ware, *Father, Son, and Holy Spirit*, 140.
2. House, *Role of Women in Ministry*, 27.
3. Ibid., 138–39
4. Ibid., 48.
5. Piper and Grudem, "Overview of Central Concerns," 66. Italics mine.
6. Ibid., 73. Italics mine.
7. Ibid., 74. Italics mine.

ered in the same category as slavery? "The existence of slavery is not rooted in any *creation ordinance*, but the existence of marriage is."[8] How can we decide what is man's work and what is woman's work? ". . . a set of criteria to help a woman think through whether the responsibilities of any given job allow her to uphold God's *created order* of mature masculinity and femininity."[9] Upon what do we base the relationships of manhood and womanhood? ". . . the relationships of manhood and womanhood . . . are rooted in the *created order*."[10]

It is clear that creation order is foundational to the complementarian argument that men have authority over women. And it appears that this understanding is based on their understanding of Genesis 1–3 and upon Paul's arguments in 1 Corinthians 11:3–8 and 1 Timothy 2:11–15.

In contrast to complementarians, egalitarians see nothing within the creation narrative that places limitations on the authority and ministry options for women. "A biblical understanding of human equality should begin with Genesis 1:26–28, where women and men together and without distinction are declared to be created in God's image and are given authority over all creation."[11] Egalitarians see this as the foundation for male/female equality, not a hierarchical relationship between men and women because of creative order. Gilbert Bilezikian not only does not read a hierarchical structure regarding men and women into the creation story, he believes the purpose of the narrative is "to show that both man and woman were uniquely made of the same human substance and that, as a result, they enjoyed, prior to the fall, a relation of full mutuality in equality."[12]

---

8. Ibid., 65. Italics mine.

9. Piper, "Biblical Complementarity," 51. Italics mine.

10. Piper and Grudem, "Overview of Central Concerns," 75. Italics mine.

11. Groothuis, "Equal in Being," 305–6.

12. Bilezikian. *Beyond Sex Roles*, 31.

Another theologian who shares the egalitarian perspective is Kevin Giles. Giles does not believe that in 1 Corinthians 11 Paul is setting forth a rationale for the permanent subordination of women based on the creation narrative in Genesis 2. In fact he questions whether being created second has any meaning whatsoever.[13] Surprisingly, among the commentators Giles quotes is John Calvin. Although Calvin sees women as inferior to men and believes they should be in subjection, he says, "Yet the reason which Paul assigns, that woman was second in the order of creation, appears not to be a very strong argument in favour of her subjection; for John the Baptist was before Christ in the order of time, and yet was greatly inferior in rank."[14] Giles says, "It is true that according to Genesis woman was created second, but nothing should be made of this descriptive observation because nothing is made of it in Genesis.[15]

As we have seen, one of the ways complementarians support their case for the subordination of women is to cite the order of creation. Their reasoning is that men were created before women and because of that men have more authority than women and it is up to women to follow male leadership. Unlike complementarians, egalitarians do not see that a hierarchical relationship between men and women is inherent in the creation narrative. Instead they see in the creation story a description of both men and women as created in the image of God and a mandate for both men and women to have authority over the rest of creation. Giles goes so far as to suggest that if the order of creation argument calling for the subordination of women could be shown to be "a human construct read back into the text of Scripture, the whole contemporary case for the permanent subordination of women would collapse. It would be seen to be an edifice without a foundation."[16]

13. Giles, *Trinity,* 171–2.
14. Calvin, *Timothy, Titus, and Philemon,* 68.
15. Giles, *Trinity,* 171–2.
16. Ibid.

The significance—or lack of significance—of creation order is a major point of contention between complementarians and egalitarians. Both sides believe the creation story helps support their perspective. While the order of creation argument is troubling, a more complicated source of conflict is the disagreement regarding permanent functional subordination. The issue of functional subordination goes beyond the relationship between men and women. It goes to our very concept of God and the Trinity

FUNCTIONAL SUBORDINATION

As I mentioned earlier, the first time I encountered the concept of essential equality and permanent functional subordination was in the late 1970s when I read George W. Knight's book, *The New Testament Teaching on the Role Relationship of Men and Women*. At the time it troubled me, but I put the issue aside, partly because I was not aware of any theologians taking issue with Knight's ideas and partly because I had my hands full with three young children and a budding writing career. It was years later that I finally encountered a full-blown critique of the functional subordination Knight advocated.

When complementarians make the case for permanent functional subordination, they are careful to explain that their perspective does not impact the deity of the Son or equality in regard to essence of being. But it is sometimes difficult to discern where the line is drawn between functional and essential equality. Knight mentions the incarnation of Christ as an example of the subordination of the Son, but he also sees Christ as subordinate because he is eternally and ontologically the son in a father/son relationship.[17] He uses the term *chain of subordination* and it is not altogether clear whether he sees an *eternal* chain of subordination in regard to the Trinity, or whether he is referring here only to

17. Knight, *New Testament Role Relationships,* 55–56.

Jesus' role on earth.[18] When he refers to ontological preincarnate submission,[19] he seems to be going beyond functional subordination or relational differentiation to something that suggests eternal ontological subordination within the Godhead.

Wayne House maintains that in the current debate regarding the role of women, there is a misunderstanding about functional relationships and personhood. He says that Paul uses the words head, submission, and exercising authority to define male and female "*functional relationships* in the home and in the gathering of believers, *not* in describing their *personhood and equality* before God."[20] House recognizes a distinct split between essence and function that allows for permanent equality of essence alongside permanent functional subordination.

Bruce Ware, another complementarian theologian, says that "the oneness of God, and hence the full essential equality of the Father, the Son, and the Holy Spirit, is constituted precisely in a oneness of divine nature possessed fully, simultaneously, and eternally by each of the divine Persons."[21] While he understands the persons of the Godhead to be essentially one, in regard to roles he says that "what distinguishes the Father from the Son and each of them from the Spirit is instead the particular roles each has within the Trinity."[22] For Ware, distinction of roles within the Trinity is marked by a hierarchical ordering. He says that, "the eternal and inner-trinitarian Father-Son relationship is marked, among other things, by an authority and submission structure in which the Father is eternally in authority over the Son and the Son eternally

18. Ibid., 33.

19. Ibid., 56.

20. House, *Role of Women in Ministry,* 29. Italics in this quote are House's.

21. Ware, "Equal in Essence," 1.

22. Ibid.

in submission to the Father."[23] The Father and the Son are equal in the essence of their being, but the Son is subordinate in role.

The complementarian argument for permanent functional subordination within the Godhead and between men and women creates a confusing hierarchical structure that seems to hinder rather than to help communicate the equality, unity, and community inherent in the Trinity and the body of Christ. While I agree that a difference in function need not imply inequality or inferiority, I do not think it is the case the way complementarians use the term function to mean a permanent subordinate position or rank. Although role submission by itself does not indicate inequality, the way complementarians use the term is unusual and more akin to a position or permanent rank than to a role or function.

Rebecca Merrill Groothuis is an articulate egalitarian who takes issue with complementarians and recognizes that the distinction they make between being (essence) and role (function) is foundational to their doctrine of male leadership. "The distinction between equal being and unequal role serves as the hermeneutical lens through which the biblical data are interpreted."[24] She describes this careful and decisive distinction between essence and function as the "theoretical construct" that allows complementarians to "interpret the submission texts as universal statements on the creational 'roles' of manhood and womanhood, while also acknowledging biblical teaching on the spiritual and ontological equality of man and woman."[25]

Groothuis is troubled by the way complementarians use the word *role*. She says, "A role is a part that is played or a particular function or office that is assumed for a specific purpose or period of time. Anyone with the requisite abilities can play the part."[26] Although her definition is not the only way to define role, it does

23. Ibid.
24. Groothuis, "Equal in Being," 303.
25. Ibid.
26. Ibid., 318

point out a significant weakness in the way the word is used by complementarians. "By definition a role is not synonymous with or inexorably tied to who a person is. Yet [for complementarians] the 'roles' of male authority and female subordination are deemed essential to God's creational design for true manhood and womanhood."[27] Groothuis says that in the normal sense of meaning, roles are limited in scope, duration, and criterion.

While it is true that there can be equality of personhood and functional subordination in role, it is questionable whether it can be true in terms of a *permanently fixed* role. According to Groothuis, the female subordination complementarians espouse is "comprehensive (encompassing all that a woman does), permanent (extending throughout the life of a woman and applying to all women at all times) and decided solely by an unchangeable aspect of a woman's personal being (femaleness)."[28] Groothuis goes on to say that used in this way the word role is basically synonymous with *being*."[29] As someone has said, there is no cash value in the equality espoused.

Groothuis does not spend a lot of time comparing the relationship between men and women with the relationship within the Godhead. But she notes that any such comparison would not indicate a subordinate role for women. She points out that if the relationships were actually comparable, there would never be any circumstances in which men would willfully overrule the will of women and wives would always fully and truly understand and support their husbands' decisions. This is frequently not the case. She concludes that since the persons of the Trinity have oneness of will, and men and women do not, the relationship of the Father and Son within the Trinity cannot be used as an illustration supporting the subordination of women.[30] Groothuis goes on to say

27. Ibid., 318–19.
28. Ibid., 316.
29. Ibid., 320.
30. Ibid., 330–31.

that "an eternal 'role' subordination of the Son to the Father not only is rife with logical and theological difficulties but utterly fails as an analogy to woman's subordination."[31] While I agree that because of the separate wills of men and women any comparison between the male/female relationship and the relationships within the Trinity is fraught with difficulty, I don't think we can ignore the way Paul linked the two relationships in 1 Corinthians 11, when he describes God as the head of Christ and man as the head of woman. He is trying to say *something*.

In *Beyond Sex Roles*, egalitarian theologian Gilbert Bilezikian, addresses this issue. He believes that in passages referring to God as the head of Christ, it is a mistake to define *head* as ruler. "God and Christ are both persons within the one being of the Trinity. Nowhere in the Bible is there a reference to a chain of command within the Trinity."[32] He goes on to say that "'subordinationist' theories were propounded during the fourth century and were rejected as heretical."[33] He says that when Christ acts in obedience to the Father it is because of his "self-assumed destiny as suffering-servant. . . . He did not learn obedience *because* He was a Son but *in spite of* the fact that He was a Son ('*although* he was a Son he learned obedience' [Heb 5:8–9])."[34] Bilezikian sees that Christ submitted in spite of his sonship, not because of it and he makes no room for eternal subordination within the Trinity.

Complementarians such as Knight, Grudem, and Ware make a case for the subordination of women by separating equality of essence from equality of function. They claim that the Father and Son within the Trinity are equal in essence, but that the Son is eternally subordinate in function. Similarly, they claim that women are equal to men in the essence of their beings, but are permanently subordinate in role or function. In contrast to complementarians, egalitar-

---

31. Ibid., 332.
32. Bilezikian, *Beyond Sex Roles,* 279n.
33. Ibid.
34. Ibid. Italics in this quote are Bilezikian's.

ians do not make a distinction between essence and function when it comes to equality. They see the relationship between the Father and the Son in the Godhead, as well as the relationship between men and women, as equal in function as well as in essence.

While the debate about permanent functional subordination may seem like an abstract theological concept or an irrelevant doctrinal issue, egalitarians would argue that it is often used to limit the ways in which women are allowed to minister or the voice they are allowed to have in their homes and churches.

SUBMISSION AND AUTHORITY

The concept of functional subordination allows complementarians to espouse equality for women on the one hand while at the same time placing limits on their spiritual authority. As we shall see, sometimes they put authority issues through a very fine sieve.

Knight believes women are not allowed to teach or lead in the church, but he lays no such restriction on praying and prophesying, which are assumed in 1 Corinthians 11. Knight explains that public prayer "does not imply or involve any authority or headship over others."[35] In the same way, he believes it is OK for women to prophesy because "prophesying, an activity in which the one prophesying is essentially a passive instrument through which God communicates, does not necessarily imply or involve authority or headship over others."[36] In a parenthetical statement he says, "compare, if we may be permitted a hopefully inoffensive note of humor, Balaam's ass [Numbers 22:22ff.]."[37] Inoffensive?

Knight is consistent in backing up his point of view regarding the role of women with biblical passages he believes are relevant, and he does acknowledge the point of view of those who see things differently. However, his perspective is based on specific passages

35. Knight, *New Testament Role Relationships*, 46.
36. Ibid., 46.
37. Ibid., 46.

which form a grid through which he views the whole of scripture. He refers to these as didactic passages that must be given precedence in order to interpret the Bible properly.[38]

Knight insists that men and women are equal but have different roles.[39] While there is no contradiction between equality and different roles, for Knight different roles for women entails subordination. Just as he sees a chain of subordination within the Trinity, he believes women have a subordinate function in relationship to men. This subordinate function places limits on women in regard to leadership and ministry.

Bruce Ware is another complementarian theologian who stresses submission and places limitations on women's ministry roles. He says, "Men and women are fully equal in essence, worth, value, and dignity, even though God has ordained that there be male headship in our relations in the home and in the church. Equality of essence does not conflict with distinction of roles."[40] He firmly grounds this perception of the authority/submission relationship between men and women in the structure of the Trinity. He says this impacts church as well as marriage. "As the Son submits eternally to the Father, and as the Spirit submits to the Father and the Son, so we are to reflect this same reality in our marriages and our churches."[41]

Ware sees this hierarchical structure as key to the Trinity. "The most marked characteristic of the Trinitarian relationships is the presence of an eternal and inherent expression of authority and submission."[42] While Ware maintains that the Father, Son, and Holy Spirit are equal and that all three fully possess the divine nature, he nevertheless insists that within the Trinity "authority and

---

38. Ibid., 29.
39. Ibid., 57.
40. Ware, *Father, Son, and Holy Spirit*, 139.
41. Ibid., 150
42. Ibid., 137.

submission are themselves eternal realities."[43] In regard to prayer he says that all prayer should be addressed to the Father who has "absolute and uncontested supremacy, including authority over the Son and the Spirit."[44]

Ware sees within the Trinity an eternal subordination of function of the Son and the Spirit to the Father. And he believes that wives can benefit "enormously from the doctrine of the Trinity in realizing that the submission required of them as wives is itself reflective of the very submission eternally given by the Son to his Father, and by the Spirit to the Father and the Son."[45] Ware believes the eternal submission of the Son to the Father sets a pattern for men and women that calls for a fixed relationship of female submission and male authority.

In contrast to Knight and Ware, egalitarian Rebecca Groothuis is adamant that women and men share spiritual authority. She understands spiritual authority as something endowed upon both men and women at creation and reinforced in the new covenant. She notes that in Genesis 1:26–28 God gave accountability and authority to both men and women, that in Galatians 3:26–28, men and women are on equal ground before God, that in 1 Peter 3:7 men and women inherit God's grace equally, and that according to 1 Peter 2:5, 9 and Revelation 1:26 and 5:10 men and women together form God's new priesthood. She says that if these things are true, there is no reason for anyone to take "spiritual responsibility for anyone else."[46] Groothuis's reading of scripture gives her a vision for both men and women that is broad and empowering. She does not see women's place as more limited than men's, but instead understands that in the New Covenant both men and women are endowed with spiritual authority.

---

43. Ibid., 157.
44. Ibid., 153.
45. Ibid., 145.
46. Groothuis, *"Equal in Being,"* 312–13.

Perhaps more than any other current theologian, Kevin Giles has attempted to break down the argument that there can be equality of essence and at the same time a permanent subordination in function. He does not believe this is the historic orthodox view of the church and makes a strong case for equality in both essence and function.

One of the things that first attracted me to Giles's writing was his treatment of Philippians 2:5–11. As I mentioned in chapter 1, Philippians 2 was the passage that allowed me to put the whole "submission" issue to rest for many years. Giles was the first theologian I encountered who related Philippians 2 to the gender debate. Giles relates Jesus' temporary, willing submission during the incarnation to the practical matter of female submission within a patriarchal culture. He advocates living out a Christlike attitude in a fallen world. Because he clearly articulates a truth I had glimpsed a number of years earlier, I will quote him at length.

> In the historically developed orthodox tradition, one text more than any other, Philippians 2:5–11, has been taken to disclose the right way to understand the whole "scope" of scripture in regard to the Son. He is eternally equal with God, yet he voluntarily and temporarily subordinated himself in the incarnation for the salvation of men and women. . . . Little has been made of this text in the contemporary debate about the status and ministry of women. Perhaps this passage points us to the most basic insight in scripture on this matter as well. Preserving one's privileges, holding on to power, is not Christlike. What is Christlike is to subordinate oneself in the service of others, whether we are male or female. If this is the ideal, then the apostle's exhortations to women to be subordinate are to be understood simply as practical advice to women living in a patriarchal culture. These directives are temporal in nature, and the response expected is voluntary. If this is so, then Paul's words to the Philippians indicate that neither the eternal subordination of the Son nor the permanent subordination of women are endorsed by the apostle.[47]

---

47. Giles, *Trinity,* 116–17.

I can hardly put into words how refreshing and affirming it was for me to come across this quote by Giles. Until I read his book, I had never heard the term subordinationism and didn't know there was a significant theological debate surrounding the subordination issue I had first encountered in George Knight's book back in the 1970s. Giles acknowledges that during the incarnation Jesus was subordinate to the Father. But, similar to the understanding with which I grew up and still believe, Giles sees this as a temporary submission during Jesus' time on earth, not an eternal subordination within the Godhead. Likewise, he does not see women as permanently subordinate to men. Instead, he understands that women living in a patriarchal culture may find it practical to voluntarily submit themselves in a Christlike manner rather than insisting upon their rights and privileges as redeemed women created in the image of God.

Somewhere in between complementarians such as Ware, who suggest that authority and submission are the most distinctive marks of Trinitarian relationship[48] and egalitarians such as Giles who believe that the functional subordination argument is only being raised to justify subordination of women,[49] are theologians such as Millard Erickson. In his book, *God in Three Persons*, Erickson—like both complementarians and egalitarians—understands that relationships within the Trinity are marked by self-sacrifice and love.[50] He says that if we attempt to pattern our family relationships on the Trinity "there will certainly not be quite the sort of patriarchalism that has sometimes characterized the family."[51] At the same time he says that in regard to our families we cannot ignore "the possibility and at least to some extent, the necessity, of something of the functional subordination that is found among

48. Ware, *Father, Son, and Holy Spirit,* 137.
49. Giles, *Trinity,* 109.
50. Erickson, *God in Three Persons,* 331.
51. Ibid., 334.

members of the Trinity."[52] But if the Trinity is marked by some manner of functional subordination, it is also marked by mutual submission. "There is therefore a mutual submission of each to each of the others and a mutual glorifying of one another. There is complete equality of the three. There has been, to be sure temporary subordination of one member of the Trinity to the other, but this is functional rather than essential."[53] Although Erickson sees some subordination within the Trinity, his arguments are finely nuanced. He says that, "this unity and equality do not require identity of function."[54] He sees the Son's subordination as temporary and understands that although there are distinct roles, "all participate in the function of each."[55] No doubt there are numerous other current theologians whose views range between stalwart complementarians such as Grudem and Ware and outspoken egalitarians such as Groothuis and Giles.

SUMMARY

In this chapter we have looked at several current theologians who make a case for the subordination of women. House, Knight, Ware, Piper, Grudem, and other complementarian theologians support their case by separating equality of essence from equality of function. The arguments put forth by these theologians are typical of others who support the complementarian point of view. They understand there is a parallel between the relationship of the Father and the Son within the Trinity and the relationship between men and women. While they acknowledge that men and women are equal in essence, as the Father and the Son are equal in essence, they maintain that there is an authority/submission structure when it comes to function. In fact, Wayne Grudem claims that without

52. Ibid., 334.
53. Ibid., 331.
54. Ibid.
55. Ibid.

the authority/submission relationship within the Godhead there would be no distinction between them. "The heresy of subordinationism, which holds that the Son is inferior in being to the Father, should be clearly distinguished from the orthodox doctrine that the Son is eternally subordinate to the Father in role or function: without this truth, we would lose the doctrine of the Trinity, for we would not have any eternal personal distinctions between the Father and the Son, and they would not eternally be Father and Son."[56] Grudem is suggesting that difference or distinction necessitates hierarchy and subordination.[57] This appears to be a major weakness of the complementarian argument. It simply is not true that distinction requires subordination. One can be distinct without being ranked above or below another.

In contrast to complementarians, egalitarians believe that equality of essence and equality of function go together. While it is possible for a person to have a subordinate role and still be equal in the essence of his or her being, it is not possible to be both equal in essence and *permanently* subordinate in role. Egalitarians believe that neither the permanent subordination of women, nor the eternal subordination of the Son within the Trinity, is logical or biblical.

Egalitarians and complementarians are opposing forces in the current debate among theologians regarding the role of women. Although there are many more theologians I could have cited on both sides of the debate, in this chapter I selected a few whose views I believe represent each side fairly.

In the next chapter we will trace the history of subordination from New Testament times to the twentieth century. It is easy to get enmeshed in the current debate and forget that these issues are not new. Tradition and the teaching of the Church play significant roles in how we interpret scripture and in the development of our Christian cultural and social norms.

56. Grudem, *Systematic Theology*, 245n.
57. Ibid., 251.

3

Orthodoxy: Who Defines It?

I CONSIDER myself a thinker, not necessarily a scholar. If I were a
real scholar I would not throw up my hands and say, "Oh, whatever," the way I do when I am stymied or tired of a topic. However,
I have continued to wrestle with one topic—the "headship" of God
as it relates to the "headship" of males—for thirty some years. It
is true I called "time-out" for twenty years or so, shrugging my
shoulders and sighing, "Whatever." But something reignited my
interest a few years ago and I have been mulling it over ever since.
The something that requickened my interest was the book by Kevin
Giles I mentioned in the previous chapter. I related to Giles's book
in several ways, one of the most significant being his application of
Philippians 2:5–11. I will come back to that in later chapters. But
in this chapter I want to explore Christian orthodoxy, something
Giles claims supports the egalitarian perspective.

The orthodox Christian view is the conventional set of beliefs
held by Christians down through the ages. But who determines
what is orthodox and what is not? The previous chapter focused on
the current debate in regard to creation order, headship, and ministry limitations. But in addition to those theological arguments,
there is a broader issue about which egalitarians and complementarians disagree. They disagree whether the orthodox Christian
view down through the centuries has been that the Son is functionally subordinate to the Father or if the early Church Fathers
and those setting forth church creeds and establishing orthodox
doctrines considered the Father and Son equal in both essence and
function.

To be subordinated is to be placed below another in power or importance. Subordination*ism*, on the other hand, often refers to a distinct doctrine, the view that there is a hierarchy within the Trinity and that the Son is eternally and ontologically subordinate to the Father. Most evangelicals would agree that this type of subordinationism, the belief that the Son is eternally subordinate to the Father in the essence of his being, was proposed in the fourth century and condemned as heretical. At the same time, many evangelicals claim that *functional* subordination is part of our orthodox evangelical heritage.[1] Everyone agrees the Son was subordinate to the Father during his incarnation. The current debate is between those who insist that the Son is eternally equal to the Father in both essence and function and those who say that although the Son is eternally equal to the Father in the essence of his being, he is eternally subordinate in function and authority.

Some complementarians insist that sonship, begotteness, and "being sent" all imply subordination and indicate that the Son has less inherent authority than the Father. In addition, they believe it is possible for the Son to be eternally equal to the Father in essence while being eternally subordinate in function. In regard to the separation between functional and essential equality it is important to note that the Church Fathers used various terms, such as acts, works, and operations, to describe the functions of the Father, Son, and Holy Spirit within the Trinity. I am using those terms interchangeably and will argue that equality of works and operations rule out functional subordination.

As I researched early theologians I focused on their views of (1) sonship, begotteness, and being sent, (2) power and authority, and (3) functional unity and equality. Although there is considerable overlap among these topics, it was important to me to see how early theologians addressed each of them. This chapter will cover the early years of the church when the Trinitarian doctrine was first articulated and set forth in church creeds. Chapter 4 will de-

1. Schreiner, "Head Coverings," 129.

scribe how the doctrine was preserved and communicated during and following the Reformation.

THE DEVELOPMENT OF CHURCH DOCTRINE

One of the most critical issues the early church faced was the development of church doctrine. Those early years were marked by debates, persecutions, heresies, religious abuse, and the formation of various creeds. Today we hold the doctrine of the Trinity as a basic tenet of Christianity. But one of the challenges of the early church was to formulate this doctrine in a way that upheld the deity of Christ without threatening the Old Testament belief that God is One. The doctrine of the Trinity is not spelled out in scripture and disputes in the early church abounded as theologians went from one extreme to another, sometimes defining God as three loosely connected Gods (Tri-theism) and at other times melding the Father, Son, and Holy Spirit into one God who manifested himself in different modes (Modalism).[2]

The doctrine of the Trinity was fluid in the years leading up to the Council of Nicea in 325. In a paper regarding authority and submission within the Trinity, complementarian Bruce Ware says that, "While the early church embraced, in time, the full essential equality of the three Trinitarian Persons, nonetheless the church has affirmed likewise the priority of the Father over the Son and Spirit."[3] Ware's statement that the church has affirmed the priority of the Father over the Son and Spirit calls for close examination. Among others, Ware quotes theologians such Tertullian to support his contention that there is an eternal authority-submission structure within the Trinity.[4] However, as P.P. Enns notes, the assumptions and speculations of Tertullian and several other very early theologians actually contributed to the Arian heresy: "Arian

2. P. P. Enns, *Moody Handbook*, 199.

3. Ware, "Equal in Essence," 9.

4. Ibid., 9–10.

doctrine had its roots in Tertullian, who subordinated the Son to the Father. . . . This ultimately led to Arianism, which denied the deity of Christ . . . . Arius and his teaching were condemned at the Council of Nicea in A.D. 325."[5]

Moving away from Arianism and the subordinationist doctrines of some other early speculative theologians, the creed developed at Nicea in A.D. 325 stressed the equality of the Father and the Son and the deity of Christ, stating that Christ was "the only-begotten of the Father, that is of the substance [ousias] of the Father, God from God, light from light, true God from true God, begotten, not made, of one substance [homoousian] with the Father."[6] The Creed of Nicea is widely recognized as foundational to Christian orthodoxy in regard to the Trinity. It is important to note that the term *homoousios*, meaning of the *same* substance is used, rather than *homoiusios*, meaning of a *similar* substance. The Arians preferred the term *homoiusios*.

Although the Creed of Nicea underscored the unity of the Godhead and the deity of Christ, debate continued, particularly in regard to the word *homoousia*, a term that some believed did not offer enough distinction among the persons of the Godhead and that implied modalism.[7] In A.D. 381 another council was convened and a slightly modified creed, the Nicene Creed, was adopted. In addition to upholding use of the term *homoousian*, the Nicene Creed confirmed the full divinity of the Holy Spirit.[8] These early creeds are generally considered foundational elements of the orthodox Christian faith.

5. Enns, *Moody Handbook*, 199.

6. Ibid., 420.

7. Giles, *Trinity*, 36.

8. Ibid., 45.

SONSHIP, BEGOTTENESS, AND BEING SENT

Both complementarians and egalitarians consider the Creed of
Nicea and the Nicene Creed to be critical documents outlining orthodox doctrine. And interestingly, both egalitarians and complementarians use them to support their points of view. This is possible
because they come to the creeds with different assumptions. In
contrast to egalitarians, complementarians assume that concepts
such as sonship, begotteness, and *being sent* indicate subordination. Egalitarians on the other hand believe that these concepts in
and of themselves simply indicate aspects of Trinitarian relationship having to do with distinctions of function, not subordination
or lesser authority.[9] Since complementarians and egalitarians see
this so differently, I was eager to see what early theologians actually had to say about begotteness and sonship.

Augustine pointed out that references to the Son being sent
by the Father and begotten of the Father do not suggest subordination or inequality: "As, therefore, the Father begat, the Son is begotten; so the Father sent, the Son was sent. But in like manner as
He who begat and He who was begotten, so both He who sent and
He who was sent, are one, since the Father and the Son are one."[10]
He said that "since the Father sent Him by a word, His being sent
was the work of both the Father and His Word; therefore the same
Son was sent by the Father and the Son, because the Son Himself
is the Word of the Father."[11] Augustine stressed the indivisibility
of both the substance and works of the Godhead and argued that
being sent or begotten did not indicate that one member of the
Godhead is greater and one is lesser.[12] Basil (330–97) understood

9. I am indebted to Giles for clarification of several of these terms that often
cause confusion and misunderstanding in regard to subordinationism. For
instance, a role is a part one plays or a function one assumes, not an essential
aspect of one's being. "Roles can change." Giles, *Jesus and the Father,* 45–54.

10 Augustine, *On the Trinity*, IV.29.

11. Augustine, *On the Trinity,* II.9.

12. Ibid., IV.32.

that the phrase "begotten, not made," suggested equal glory.[13] A later theologian indicated that the word begotten suggested common substance rather than subordination or a spin-off of some sort.[14] Being sent and being begotten are matters of distinction and identification, not subordination.

Augustine also consistently points out that *sonship* does not necessitate inferiority or subordination. He says that "the Son is not less, but it is simply intimated that He is of the Father, in which words not His inequality but His birth is declared."[15] We can even see this illustrated on the human level. For instance, would we say that the authority of Jesse was greater than his son David? That the role of Moses' unnamed father was greater than his? That Abraham remained subordinate to his father Terah? We can see then, that when Augustine explains how the persons of the Trinity are differentiated as Father, Son, and Holy Spirit, he is defending both equality and diversity within the Godhead, not suggesting subordination. Although authority and submission characterize a father/*child* relationship for a given time or in certain circumstances, they are not the defining characteristics of earthly father/*son* relationships, much less relationships within the Trinity. Mark Strauss, an advocate for inclusive language, explains why it is not accurate to substitute *child* for *son* in gender inclusive biblical translations. Although he is speaking to a different issue, the point he makes is significant. "The use of 'Child' could carry implications of immaturity that 'Son' does not. Jesus is the mighty Son of God in all the glory and magnificence of his exaltation as heir of all things (see Heb 1:3). He is not an immature child."[16]

This is in contrast to those who believe that the Father and Son relationship is inherently one of submission and authority and

13. Basil, *On the Holy Spirit*, 31.

14. Warfield says, "The adjective 'only begotten' conveys the idea, not of derivation and subordination, but of uniqueness and consubstantiality: Jesus is all that God is, and He alone is this." Warfield, *Person and Work*, 56.

15. Augustine, *On the Trinity*, II.3.

16 Strauss, *Distorting Scripture*, 181.

that it is this submissive/authoritative aspect of their relationship that primarily differentiates the members of the Godhead from one another.[17] Although Augustine repeatedly states that being sent and being begotten are relationship distinctions rather than matters of less or greater, Ware insists that the Son's being sent indicates the Father's authority. "Yes, indeed . . . the Son as from the Father is under the authority of his Father, having come to earth to become incarnate precisely because he was sent from the Father to become a man."[18] For Augustine, the sending of the Son was a joint endeavor involving both the Father and the Son. It was about diversity, equality, and unity not authority and submission. But for a number of current theologians, the sending of the Son is a matter of the Father's authority over the Son.

Augustine and Basil are two influential early theologians who maintained that sonship, begotteness, and being sent do not indicate inequality or subordination, but instead argue for oneness and unity. Far from advocating the functional subordination of the Son, Augustine and Basil argue that the relationship between the Father and the Son is marked by unity and equality.

POWER AND AUTHORITY

At the time the early creeds were developed, and shortly thereafter, many theologians attempted to formulate statements about the Trinity to help explain the unique relationship in a way that protected both the unity of the Godhead and the distinctives of the Father, Son, and Holy Spirit. Of particular interest here is whether

17. Ware says that the distinction of persons in the Godhead is "manifest by the inherent authority of the Father and inherent submission of the Son." Bruce Ware, "*Equal in Essence*," 10. Grudem makes this same point, assuming the Father/Son relationship is necessarily one of authority/submission. Grudem, *Systematic Theology*, 251. Also, Grudem sees the authority/submission relationship within the Trinity as the "means by which Father, Son, and Holy Spirit differ from one another and can be differentiated from one another." Grudem, *Evangelical Feminism*, 433.

18. Ware, "Equal in Essence," 12.

it was understood that the Son was equal to the Father in power and authority. Although there is a slight difference in meaning, I am assuming that unless specified otherwise, references to God's power also reference His authority.[19]

In the fight against Arianism, Athanasius (300–373), stands out as a defender of the deity of Christ.[20] Athanasius pointed out that although it is true that during the incarnation Jesus submitted himself to the Father, when it came to the resurrection, the Son raised his own body—that he was an active, rather than a passive, participant. He said that no one should doubt that "He is very Son of God, having His being from God as from a Father, Whose Word and wisdom and Whose Power He is."[21] Athanasius saw the Father and the Son united in their power and understood that the work of the Son included creation as well as redemption.

In *On the Holy Spirit*, Basil, another early theologian (330–97), also affirms the equality of Christ's power. Writing in response to the argument that the Son received commandments from the Father in a way that would suggest his inferiority, Basil says, "He shines forth from the Father, and accomplishes everything according to His Parent's plan. He is not different in essence, nor is He different in power from His Father, and if their power is equal, then their works are the same."[22] Basil affirms that the Father and the Son are the same in their power and works. It is difficult to imagine that Basil would support the idea that the Son is equal to the Father in essence, but permanently subordinate in function or works.[23]

19. The dictionary definition of power is "to do, act, or produce . . . the ability to control others; authority." At the same time, the definition of authority is "the power to give commands, enforce obedience, take action, or make final decisions." For the most part, power assumes authority and authority assumes power. *Webster's New World College Dictionary*, 95.

20. Giles, *Trinity*, 33–34.

21. Athanasius, *On the Incarnation*, 63–64.

22 Basil, *On the Holy Spirit*, 39.

23. Basil emphasized the voluntary nature of the Son's role in redemption.

Some complementarians complain that egalitarians don't deal with biblical passages describing eternal relationship and authority differences within the Trinity. "Nor do they deal with 1 Corinthians 15:28 or the many passages in the epistles that indicate that the Son intercedes before the Father, that the Son is seated at the right hand of the Father, and that it is the Father's throne—passages that indicate that the Son will be subject to the authority of the Father for all eternity."[24] However, egalitarians do not ignore these passages. Instead they follow the lead of fourth century theologians such as Basil. Basil said that being seated at the right hand of the Father (Heb 1:3) is not a seat of inferiority—"The expression 'right hand' does not indicate a lower place as they contend, but a relationship of equality. . . . It remains for our opponents to explain how this phrase indicates inferior rank."[25] Both Athanasius and Basil take pains to explain that the Father and the Son are eternally united and equal in rank, power, and works.

About three hundred years after Athanasius and Basil, John of Damascus (c.675–c.749) wrote a work titled *Fountain of Wisdom*, including a section called, "An Exact Exposition of the Orthodox Faith." His purpose was to "collate and epitomize in a single work the opinions of the great ecclesiastical writers who have gone before him."[26] His book, *Concerning the Orthodox Faith*, has been described as the most important of his writings and "one of the most notable works of Christian antiquity." It is an "inexhaustible thesaurus of tradition which became the standard for the great

---

"We must not think that the salvation the Son has won for us is the result of a slave's compulsory and subordinate service. No, He voluntarily accomplishes His plan out of goodness and compassion for His creation, fulfilling the Father's will. We follow true religion if we bear witness to the Son's power made manifest in everything He has fulfilled and accomplished, never separating His work from the Father's will." Basil, *On the Holy Spirit*, 37.

24. Grudem, *Evangelical Feminism*, 425.

25. Basil, *On the Holy Spirit*, 30.

26. *Catholic Encyclopedia*, s.v. "Saint John Damascene."

Scholastics who followed."[27] In a chapter on the Trinity, John of Damascus says that the unity of the persons of the Trinity in regard to authority is demonstrated by their "being identical in authority and power and goodness . . . . For there is one essence, one goodness, one power, one will, one energy, one authority, one and the same, I repeat, not three resembling each other."[28]

It seems significant that in a work, the purpose of which was to *epitomize* the opinions of the early theologians, John of Damascus adamantly affirms that within the essential oneness of the Trinity there is also oneness of *authority*. How can the Father and Son be "identical in authority" and yet be differentiated by the Father's authority and the Son's submission as some claim?

Another important pre-Reformation theologian is Saint Thomas Aquinas (1225–74). Following other early theologians, Aquinas recognized the personal distinctives within the Trinity, but stressed equality within the Godhead. He was careful to make a distinction between the persons of the Trinity without suggesting one was superior or inferior to the others.[29] In a discussion regarding hierarchies among the angels he denies that there is likewise a hierarchy within the Trinity. He wrote, "For among divine persons there is a kind of natural order but no hierarchic order."[30] Aquinas does not explain here what he means by *natural order,* but in an article regarding equality among the members of the Trinity, Aquinas elaborates on his understanding of power within the Trinity. "As the same essence is paternity in the Father, and filiation in the Son, so by the same power the Father begets, and the Son is begotten. Hence it is clear that the Son can do whatever the Father can do."[31] Aquinas makes it clear that although their power

27. Ibid.

28. John of Damascus, "Concerning the Holy Trinity," Book I, Chapter VIII.

29. Aquinas, *Basic Writings,* 404.

30. Aquinas, *Treatise on the Conservation,* Q108, Art. 1.

31. Aquinas, *Basic Writings,* 412.

is the same, their roles are not interchangeable. "But it does not follow that the Son can beget, for to argue thus would imply transition from substance to relation, since generation signifies a divine relation. So the Son has the same power as the Father, but with another relation."[32] For Aquinas it is important to acknowledge an ordering among the persons of the Trinity because not to do so would discount their distinct personalities, but he does not assume that ordering necessitates functional subordination, hierarchical ranking, or a difference in power.

FUNCTIONAL UNITY AND EQUALITY

As has already been noted, Basil was one of the early theologians who recognized the equality of *power* within the Trinity and understood *begotteness* to indicate equal glory rather than subordination. He also defended the *functional equality* and unity within the Godhead. "The work of the Father is not separate or distinct from the work of the Son; whatever the Son 'sees the Father doing . . . that the Son does likewise' [John 5:19]."[33] This was Athanasius's understanding as well. As we saw in regard to power and authority, Athanasius understood that the Father and the Son work together in both creation and redemption. "There is thus no inconsistency between creation and salvation; for the One Father has employed the same Agent for both works, effecting the salvation of the world through the same Word Who made it in the beginning."[34] Although describing the Son as the *agent* of the Father hints at subordination, Athanasius saw the members of the Trinity acting together as they carried out God's work. "When the Son works, the Father is the Worker, and the Son coming to the Saints, the Father is He who cometh in the Son. . . . Therefore also . . . when the Father

32. Ibid.
33. Basil, *On the Holy Spirit*, 39.
34. Athanasius, *On the Incarnation*, 26.

gives grace and peace, the Son also gives it."[35] Athanasius saw the Father and the Son functioning together, not one in subordination to the other.

Although some current theologians repeatedly insist that biblical descriptions of the Father giving and sending indicate an authority/submission relationship between the Father and the Son,[36] Athanasius says that the Father and the Son work together. "When the Father gives grace and peace, the Son also gives it."[37] Athanasius appears to have a significantly different understanding of this than current theologians who support functional subordination within the Trinity. Athanasius maintains that the Father and the Son are united in their works as well as their essence.

We have noted that there is no debate about the Son's subordination during the incarnation. Everyone recognizes that during his time on earth the Son was in subordination to the Father. But Augustine points out that during the incarnation the Son was subordinate even to Himself. "The Son of God is both understood to be equal to the Father according to the form of God in which He is, and less than the Father according to the form of a servant which He took . . . . and not only so, but less even than Himself."[38] In his commitment to clarify the eternal equality of the members of the Trinity, Augustine points out that the Son's subordination during the incarnation was in part subordination to himself.

Likewise, Augustine insisted that Paul's statement in 1 Corinthians 15:27–28 about the Father subjecting all things to the Son does not have implications regarding a top-down subordination within the Godhead, but rather indicates an inseparable, reciprocal type of subjection. "Let him not think that the words 'He has subjected all things to the Son,' are to be understood of the Father in such a way as to think that the Son has not subjected

35. Athanasius, *Against the Arians,* III.11.

36. Ware, "Equal in Essence," 2.

37. Athanasius, *Against the Arians.,* III.11.

38. Augustine, *On the Trinity,* II.2 .

all things to Himself . . . . For the operation of the Father and the Son is inseparable."[39] In Augustine's view, the oneness of the Father and Son is so complete that if the Father is subjecting all things to Himself, the Son is participating in that act of subjecting. In another place Augustine noted that the "will of the Father and the Son is one, and their operation is inseparable."[40]

Prominent early theologians such as Augustine, Athanasius, Basil, and Aquinas described the functional equality of God the Father and God the Son and articulated that their operations could not be separated. If there is no indication of a separation between the operations of one and the operations of the other, it is difficult to see how there could be a separation between their essence and their functions.

SUMMARY

Before the Reformation, in the early years of the church, important church doctrines were hammered out in the midst of controversy, charges of heresy, ex-communications, and anathemas. During the first two and a half centuries the doctrine of the Trinity was in the development stage, so it would be surprising to find absolute agreement regarding the Trinity. But eventually a number of important creeds such as the Creed of Nicea (A.D. 325), the Apostles Creed (c. A.D. 340)[41], the Nicene Creed (A.D. 381), and the Athanasian Creed (c. A.D. 500)[42] were established to distill the experience and understanding of the early church.[43] Early theologians, and the creeds they developed, were careful to stress the oneness of the Trinity while at the same time articulating it in a way that acknowledged three separate persons within one Godhead.

---

39. Ibid., I.15, 22.
40. Ibid. II.9, 61.
41. Bettenson, *Documents*, 23–25.
42. Giles, *Trinity*, 51.
43. McGrath, *Doctrine*, 199.

The Church Fathers were primarily concerned with defending the deity of the Son and so were not necessarily addressing the issues raised in the current debate regarding functional subordination. However, in their writings there is a striking emphasis on equality and oneness within the Trinity. There is relationship, and an ordering of relationship, but unless you assume that ordering implies hierarchy, or that sonship implies less authority, there is little in these early formulations indicating eternal functional subordination of the Son to the Father. Early theologians affirm that the Father and the Son are equal in their attributes, works, word, will, thought, deeds, authority, operations, power, rank, and glory. If they are equal in all of these, then it seems the argument for subordination would have to be presumed upon something other than function.

As we will see in the next chapter, many of the creeds and doctrines formulated during the early years of church history in the midst of heated debates, heresies, and accusations of heresy, endured up to and beyond the tumultuous Reformation period.

4

Orthodoxy: Who Preserves It?

As we have seen, the doctrine of the Trinity was established in the fourth century and for the most part the equality of the Father and the Son in both essence and works was defended down through the centuries. I should point out that the focus of this debate on the relationship between the Father and the Son in no way is meant to diminish the importance of the Holy Spirit. All the persons of the Trinity are equal in both essence and function. However, because the question arises out of Paul's reference to God as the head of Christ, the debate is framed around the relationship between the Father and the Son.

At the time of the Reformation numerous theological questions were thoroughly debated, so it should be no surprise that one of the issues that surfaced was the doctrine of the Trinity. Opponents of the doctrine of the Trinity considered it unscriptural and irrational.[1] Although the doctrine itself came under attack, it does not appear that subordination within the Trinity was a major issue for those who supported the Trinitarian doctrine itself. It seems the Reformers considered equality among the members of the Trinity an issue settled by early church creeds and treated it as a given.[2] In this chapter we will look at how this doctrine was understood during the Reformation and on down through the twentieth century.

1. Gonzalez, *Christian Thought*, 101–2.
2. Giles, *Trinity*, 167.

In his commentary on 1 Corinthians, John Calvin acknowledges both ordering and equality within the Trinity, but notes that any implied subordination is restricted to Jesus' incarnation. "God, then, occupies the *first* place: Christ holds the *second* place. How so? Inasmuch as he has in our flesh made himself subject to the Father, for, apart from this, being of one essence with the Father, he is his equal."[3] Calvin went on to say that Christ was "inferior to the Father, inasmuch as he assumed our nature."[4]

In the *Institutes*, Calvin again refers to the relationship between the Father and the Son, this time in regard to the future. "But when . . . we shall see God as he is, then Christ, having accomplished the office of Mediator, shall cease to be the vicegerent of the Father, and will be content with the glory which he possessed before the world was."[5] It seems clear that Calvin perceived the "headship" of the Father—whether in essence or function—as temporal, not eternal. "God will then cease to be the head of Christ, and Christ's own Godhead will then shine forth of itself, whereas it is now in a manner veiled."[6] Calvin understood that Jesus was subordinate during the incarnation and in his role as mediator. But that when we see God as he is, we will see that God is no longer "the head of Christ" and that the members of the Trinity are equal in their glory and majesty.

The 1619 Belgic Confession is consistent with Calvin's view. It states: "The Father was never without his Son, nor without his Holy Spirit, since all these are equal from eternity, in one and the same essence. There is neither a first nor a last, for all three are one in truth and power, in goodness and mercy."[7] This creed, similar to other reformed documents, avers that the persons of the Trinity are equal in essence as well as power.

3. Calvin, *Corinthians*, 353. Italics are Calvin's, not mine.

4. Ibid.

5. Calvin, *Institutes*, II.xiii.3.

6. Ibid.

7. *The Belgic Confession*.

For the most part, the early church doctrines and creeds in regard to the Trinity remained fast during the Reformation.[8] Although Calvin speaks of Jesus being "subject to the Father" and "inferior to the Father,"[9] it is clear within the context that he is referring to Jesus' ministry here on earth and to his role as mediator, not to an eternal functional subordination of the Son within the Godhead.[10]

ECONOMIC TRINITY

If during the Reformation the doctrine of the Trinity was attacked by certain theologians and defended by others, after the Reformation the topic of the Trinity did not command a lot of attention. "The tendency was to treat the Trinity as a formal doctrine that needed to be outlined and then left to one side."[11] Nevertheless, during this time period several theologians distinguished between the economic (as revealed to man) Trinity and the immanent (ontological, essential) Trinity.

Wayne Grudem says that when speaking of the *economy of the Trinity,* the word *economy* is used in the sense of *ordering of activities.* "The 'economy of the Trinity' means the different ways the three persons act as they relate to the world and . . . to each other for all eternity."[12] Kevin Giles explains the economic and immanent Trinity as follows: "The former refers to the Trinity as revealed in God's unfolding work of creation and redemption in history; the latter refers to the essential being of the triune God, which no human could ever completely comprehend."[13] Giles goes on to suggest that God's revelation is marked by both truth and

---

8. Giles, *Trinity,* 59.

9. Calvin, *Corinthians,* vol. 1, 353.

10. Calvin, *Institutes,* II.xiv.3.

11. Giles, *Jesus and the Father,* 168.

12. Grudem, *Systematic Theology,* 248.

13. Giles, *Trinity,* 28.

restraint. "This distinction between the immanent Trinity and the economic Trinity allows that there is more to God than what is revealed to us but that what is revealed is true and accurate. God is not other than he is in revelation"[14]

I think it would be safe to say that the economic Trinity refers to the activities of the Father, Son, and Holy Spirit as they are revealed to us in the history of creation and redemption. While the incarnation is part of that, it is not the whole story. When we consider what the Bible reveals to us about the role of the Son in creation[15] (Col 1:15–20), sanctification (Eph 5:26), judgment (2 Tim 4:1), and mediation (Heb 4:14–16), we can say with some assurance that the function of the Son within the economic Trinity is not limited to the incarnation. The function of the Son is not limited to his subordination as fleshed out in the incarnation, and the economic Trinity as a whole is not necessarily distinguished by a hierarchy of roles.

SUBORDINATION

A.H. Strong (1839–1921) maintained that subordination within the Godhead was not inconsistent with equality. "Priority is not necessarily superiority. . . .We frankly recognize an eternal subordination of Christ to the Father, but we maintain at the same time that this subordination is a subordination of order, office, and operation, not a subordination of essence"[16] Although Strong sees Christ as equal to the Father in essence, he also understands Him to be eternally subordinate to the Father in function or operation.

---

14. Ibid.

15. In regard to creation, Augustine says, "For if some things were made by the Father, and some by the Son, then all things were not made by the Father, nor all things by the Son; but if all things were made by the Father, and all things by the Son, then the same things were made by the Father and by the Son. The Son, therefore is equal with the Father, and the working of the Father and the Son is indivisible." Augustine, *On the Trinity*, 1:12.

16. Strong, *Systematic Theology*, 342.

At the same time, Strong argues that the biblical terms *generation* and *procession,* words sometimes used to make a case for the subordination of the Son, "are but approximate expressions of the truth, and we are to correct by other declarations of scripture any imperfect impressions which we might derive solely from them." He goes on to say that these terms are used in a special manner "which we explicitly state and define as excluding all notions of inequality between the persons of the Trinity."[17] While Strong decries the idea of inequality within the Trinity, he appears to support permanent functional subordination.

A further overview of the views of post-Reformation theologians indicates ambiguity and disagreement regarding subordination. Charles Hodge (1797–1878) makes a clear statement regarding the subordination of Christ in his commentary on 1 Corinthians 11:3. "The obvious meaning of this passage is, that the woman is subordinate to the man, the man is subordinate to Christ, and Christ is subordinate to God."[18] However, Hodge sometimes limited his views regarding subordination to the incarnation. "It is the incarnate Son of God, who, in the great work of redemption, is said to be subordinate to the Father, whose will he came into the world to do."[19] In regard to 1 Corinthians 15:28, a passage speaking of the future, Hodge takes pains to explain that the subjection in this passage is referring to the subjection of the incarnate Son. There is something in Hodge's thinking that distinguishes between the second person of the Trinity and the incarnate Son. If he did not limit the Son's subordination to the incarnation, he still makes a distinction between "the Son as Son" and "the Son as incarnate," and in some sense, at least, limits the subjection of the Son to the incarnation.[20]

17. Ibid., 341.
18. Hodge, *Corinthians*, 206.
19. Ibid., 207.
20 Ibid., 333–34.

UNITY AND EQUALITY

If some post-Reformation theologians waffled about the equality of the Son within the Trinity and didn't always make it clear if, when they referred to subordination, they were only referring to subordination during the incarnation, others took pains to explain how they understood subordination, the economic Trinity, and the incarnation.

Benjamin B. Warfield (1851–1921) was a professor in the Theological Seminary at Princeton from 1887 to 1921. In *The Person and Work of Christ*, Warfield points out that as the only begotten Son of God, Jesus is unique rather than subordinate. "The adjective 'only begotten' conveys the idea, not of derivation and subordination, but of uniqueness and consubstantiality: Jesus is all that God is, and He alone is this."[21] This is in contrast to Wayne Grudem who asserts that the phrase "begotten of the Father before all ages," in the Nicene Creed affirms an eternal role subordination of the Son.[22]

In addition to clarifying that "begotteness" did not necessitate subordination, Warfield asserts that the Son's coming to earth in human form was voluntary and did not reflect on his eternal standing within the Godhead. "By nature He was God; and He would have naturally lived as became God—'on an equality with God.' He became man by a voluntary act, 'taking no account of Himself,' and having become man, He voluntarily lived out His human life under the conditions which the fulfillment of His unselfish purpose imposed on Him"[23] Warfield believed that the Son came to earth voluntarily and that biblical passages referring to the Son's subordination during the incarnation did not reflect on his eternal standing. Warfield is one of the theologians Grudem cites in *Evangelicalism and Biblical Truth* to support functional sub-

---

21. Warfield, *Person and Work*, 56.
22. Grudem, *Systematic Theology*, 251.
23. Giles, *Trinity*, 107.

ordination. However, in a footnote, Grudem acknowledges that Warfield questions "how we can derive from scripture any idea of an eternal subordination of the Son to the Father . . . . Warfield does not deny the eternal subordination of the Son to the Father, but he also comes short of actually affirming it."[24]

Two other post-Reformation theologians who have weighed in regarding the Trinity are Karl Barth (1886–1968) and Karl Rahner (1904–1984). I will not pretend to have a solid understanding of the writings of either of these two theologians, but from what I have read, they both place heavy emphasis on unity within the Godhead. Barth believed the members of the Trinity acted as one. "From creation by way of revelation and reconciliation to the coming redemption it is always true that He who acts here is the Father and the Son and the Spirit."[25] Barth maintains that the three members of the Trinity act together "No attribute, no act of God is not in the same way the attribute or act of the Father, the Son and the Spirit."[26] In a discussion regarding the Son's participation in creation and redemption, Barth says, "If the Son has a share in what was called the special work of the Father, if He works with the Father in the work of creation, then this means, at least in the sense of Athanasius and the theology which finally triumphed in the fourth century, that He is of one essence with Him."[27] Far from suggesting that the Son is equal in essence but subordinate in works, Barth says that it is the Son's very participation in God's works that confirm his oneness with the Father. "In order that all things might be made by Him, in order that He might be the Mediator of creation, He Himself had to be God by nature."[28] If I understand Barth correctly, he is saying that the Son's function confirms his essential equality with the Father. Barth understands the works of the Father and the Son to be one.

24. Grudem, *Evangelical Feminism*, 420.
25. Barth, *Church Dogmatics,* 375.
26. Ibid., 362.
27. Ibid., 442
28. Ibid.

Karl Rahner was a twentieth century Catholic theologian concerned with assuring that the doctrine of the Trinity remained relevant. Writing about the use of the term "persons" in the Trinity, Rahner is concerned that it conveys too much separation. He says, "But there exists in God only *one* power, *one* will, only one self-presence, a unique activity, a unique beatitude, and so forth."[29] While holding to oneness within the Trinity, it is also necessary to make distinctions. He says that "we must say that the Father, Son, and Spirit are identical with the one godhead and are 'relatively' distinct from one another," that "these three as distinct are constituted only by their relatedness to one another," and that "in God everything is one except where there is relative opposition."[30] One of Rahner's primary concerns is to make a connection between the Trinity and man.[31] To that end he makes the statement that "The 'economic' Trinity is the 'immanent' Trinity and the 'immanent' Trinity is the 'economic' Trinity."[32] Although this statement could suggest that any subordination within the economic Trinity would mean eternal ontological subordination as well, that does not seem to be his intent. He does say that "There has occurred in salvation history something which can be predicated only of one divine person,"[33] suggesting that only the Son could have participated in the incarnation. But it is not clear that he is at the same time saying that because only the Son could have participated in the incarnation, and that during the incarnation the Son was subordinate to the Father, it means that the Son is eternally subordinated. As I said, his primary concern has more to do with making a *real* connection between the Trinity and man and he thus attempts to erase the distinction between the economic Trinity and the immanent Trinity.

29. Rahner, *Trinity*, 75.
30. Ibid., 72–73.
31. Ibid., 73.
32. Ibid., 22.
33. Ibid., 23.

SUMMARY

We have seen that in recent years there has been some ambiguity and confusion regarding subordination within the Trinity. To some it has seemed the Trinity is a doctrine Christians must adhere to in order to remain orthodox, but that it is easy to set aside as incomprehensible and irrelevant to Christian living.[34] I suspect Carl Henry speaks for many when he asks the following rhetorical question: "Is the doctrine of the Trinity a futile intellectual effort to resolve inherently contradictory notions of divine unity and divine plurality? Are orthodox evangelicals driven to say that anyone who rejects this doctrine may lose his soul whereas anyone who tries to explain it will lose his mind?"[35] The doctrine of the Trinity is unquestionably a difficult topic to explore, but it remains an important one. From New Testament times to the present, theologians have struggled to explain the Trinity in ways that elucidate the oneness of God as well as the diversity within the Godhead.

Much of the concern among orthodox theologians regarding the Trinity has been a defense of the deity of the Son and the Holy Spirit and of equality within the Godhead. Although theologians generally recognize ordering and diversity within the Trinity, and a few theologians, such as Strong and Hodge, assume this implies subordination, it has not necessarily been generally assumed that this ordering indicates permanent subordination of the Son and the Holy Spirit to the Father.

The question at hand is whether there is an eternal functional subordination of the Son to the Father. In my reading I have detected far more emphasis on equality of both essence and function within the Godhead than on functional subordination and I'm not sure that either complementarians or egalitarians can claim that their perspective on eternal functional subordination represents the timeless "orthodox Christian view." The Trinity remains a

---

34. Giles, *Jesus and the Father*, 168.

35. C. Henry, *God, Revelation and Authority*, 165.

mystery in many ways and for one side or the other to claim the ability to represent the view of all Christians for all time is questionable.[36] However, imbedded in the debate of whether there is an eternal functional subordination of the Son to the Father is a troubling question. Is it possible for the Son to be *eternally functionally* subordinate without also being *ontologically* subordinate? Eternal ontological equality is assumed by both egalitarians and complementarians. However, if the Father and Son are united in their attributes, works, word, will, thought, deeds, authority, operations, power, rank, glory, majesty, truth, goodness and mercy, as early theologians claim, then what is the basis for functional subordination?

These are not questions I can fully answer in this book, but they are critical underlying questions and I believe in large part are responsible for the current impasse between complementarians and egalitarians regarding the Trinity. Complementarians such as Grudem and Ware claim that the Son is subordinate to the Father in function and authority and that this is the historical orthodox view of the church. However, I do not see the theory of functional subordination supported by the Church Fathers or by the majority of theologians throughout the history of Christianity. I have concluded that church history does not support the eternal functional subordination of the Son within the Trinity and that the functional subordination of the Son cannot be used as an argument for the subordination of women. At the same time, I think there is something we can learn from Trinitarian relationships in regard to the relationship between men and women. In the next chapter we will turn our attention to women and to how their role has been understood from New Testament times to the present.

36. I like the idea of *perichoresis*, a circle dance in which God as three persons is in a constant circular movement that implies community, intimacy, equality, love, unity and yet distinction. Cladis, *Team-Based Church*, 4.

5

Women: What Are We Here For?

IN THE current debate regarding the role of women, complementarians maintain that women are equal to men in their essence, but subordinate in function. Many theologians in the past did not split hairs so finely. They simply considered women subordinate and inferior. This chapter will survey the status and ministry of women from New Testament times to the present. I was startled by some of the statements early theologians made about the status of women. But even while they offend my twenty-first century sensibilities, I can detect vestiges of their thinking in some of today's churches and among certain theologians.

GOD ORDAINED HIERARCHY?

The status of women is an issue in secular culture as well as in the church. Over the last fifty years the feminist movement has instigated significant upheaval in our culture regarding the role and status of women. It can be argued that feminists have had a negative impact on our culture. In a number of instances I believe that is true. I tend to associate the feminist label with anger and revolt and, while I consider myself an egalitarian, I shy away from calling myself a feminist. But the feminist movement has raised awareness about blatant discrimination and in that regard has served our culture well. I recognize I enjoy freedoms and opportunities today that I would not know if it were not for feminists who have battled on my behalf.

Secular culture increasingly recognizes the equality of women and acts to protect their rights. The religious community, however, lags behind. And there is a legitimate reason for this. In Christian circles, discrimination is not the only issue with which we must deal. We must also wrestle with God's intentions. What if God intends for women to be subordinate to men? Are we violating God's will if we break down the obstacles barring women from positions of leadership? For many years the answer to that question has been a firm, if not resounding, "Yes."

As we saw in Chapter 2, complementarians hearken back to Genesis to bolster their argument that God intended women to be subordinate to men. Early theologians did the same. For instance, Ambrose (340–97), commenting on the creation narrative, recognized the important role of women in regard to childbearing but overall considered women inferior. "If we take the word 'helper' in a good sense, then the woman's cooperation turns out to be something of major import in the process of generation, just as the earth by receiving, confining, and fostering the seed causes it to grow and produce fruit in time."[1] He noted that even though women were in an inferior position, they had their purpose and that men found them useful, just as "men in high and important offices often enlist the help of men who are below them in rank and esteem."[2] Earlier, illustrating his argument that one's status does not depend on one's place of origin, he comes to the following conclusion: "Hence, although created outside Paradise, that is, in an inferior place, man is found superior, whereas woman, created in a better place, that is to say, in Paradise, is found to be inferior."[3] He begins with the premise that men are superior to women and works backward to conclude that one's status is not determined by one's place of origin. His underlying assumption regarding the

1. Ambrose, *Hexameron*, 327.
2. Ibid.
3. Ibid., 301.

inferiority of women determines his reasoning and the illustration he chooses to make his point.

Aquinas (1225–1274) is another early theologian who assumed that women were meant to be subordinate. He believed the subjection of women was natural and that their subordinate position was determined by God before the Fall. He pointed out that there *is* such a thing as wrongful subjection, which he calls servile, in which a person uses a subject for his or her own benefit. But he understands another kind of subjection, which he calls civil or economic subjection that has the good of the subject in mind. He sees this kind of subjection as necessary and beneficial. "For the good of order would have been wanting in the human family if some were not governed by others wiser than themselves. So by such a kind of subjection woman is naturally subject to man, because in man the discernment of reason predominates."[4] In Aquinas's mind, women are to be subordinate, in some part at least, because of their inferior reasoning ability. Later, when we look at interdependency, we will see that Aquinas accorded women a measure of honor and appreciation. But here it is impossible to miss his underlying assumption that God ordained the subjection of women and that it is justified by their inherent inferiority, particularly in regard to their reasoning ability.

John Calvin, the great Reformation theologian, saw women as inferior in numerous ways. He described woman as "the distinguished *ornament* of the man" and noted that "as the woman derives her origin from man, she is therefore inferior in rank."[5] He puzzled some over the 1 Corinthians 11:7 passage where Paul describes man as the image and glory of God and woman as the glory of man, whereas Genesis 1:27 says that both male and female were created in God's image. He concluded that God has distinguished man is such a way as to "have superiority over the woman," and that in this superior order "the glory of God is seen, as it shines

4. Aquinas, *Basic Writings*, 880–81.
5. Calvin, *Corinthians,* 357. Italics are mine.

forth in every kind of superiority."[6] Men are superior, women are inferior, and God is glorified in the superior.

Matthew Henry (1661–1714), in his commentary on 1 Corinthians, summarizes what seems to be the prevalent view following the Reformation regarding male headship. He said that man's dominion over woman is not as pronounced as God's dominion over the man Jesus, "but a superiority and headship he has and the woman should be in subjection and not assume or usurp the man's place."[7] Henry P. Liddon (1829–90) said that this "priority in creation implies a certain superiority."[8] Likewise, Patrick Fairbairn (1805–74) believed that the order of creation had implications regarding "superiority in place and power."[9]

Like today's complementarian theologians, earlier theologians such as Ambrose, Aquinas, Calvin, and Henry, believed that God put women in subjection to men and that this subjection could be traced back to creation. But unlike today's complementarians, they did not make a distinction between essence and function. They simply believed that women were inherently inferior and meant to be in subjection. This was their God given status.

FEMALE SKILLS, GIFTS, AND CHARACTER

Many theologians based their assumptions regarding the subordination of women on their understanding of what the Bible taught and they did not try to explain why this should be. Others, however, saw within women themselves the rationale for their limited role.

It seems to me that Martin Luther was a practical man who brought common sense into the church during the Reformation. He is adamant about the priesthood of all believers and argued

6. Calvin, *Corinthians*, 357.

7. M. Henry, *Commentary*, 561.

8. Liddon, *Timothy*, 18–19.

9. Fairbairn, *Pastoral Epistles*, 128.

vehemently that through faith and baptism all believers are part of the priesthood and are endowed with God's power.[10] Nevertheless, he maintained that only those who are "better fitted than others," should use that power publicly. He recognized the importance of giftedness. "The person who wishes to preach needs to have a good voice, good eloquence, a good memory and other natural gifts; whoever does not have these should properly keep still and let somebody else speak."[11] Amen to that. But while arguing that those who serve as priests should be selected according to their giftedness, he also pointed out that some people, such the dumb, the handicapped, the incompetent, and women were automatically disqualified.[12] In addition to restricting from ordination persons with physical limitations, he dismisses the possibility that women could be as gifted and skilled as men. "Thus Paul forbids women to preach in the congregation where men are present who are skilled in speaking, so that respect and discipline may be maintained; because it is much more fitting and proper for a man to speak, a man is also more skilled at it."[13] Luther presumed men were better at speaking than women and assumed that this reality—plus a desire for doing things properly—was behind the Apostle Paul's restrictions regarding women preaching.

For Luther, Paul's instructions that women be silent in the church took precedence over one of his most cherished concepts—the priesthood of all believers. At the same time he allowed for exceptions. "Therefore order, discipline, and respect demand that women keep silent when men speak; but if no man were to preach, then it would be necessary for the women to preach."[14] He would also, in emergencies, allow women to baptize and hear confes-

---

10. Luther, *Works,* vol. 40, 21.
11. Ibid., vol. 36, 151.
12. Ibid.
13. Luther, *Works,* vol. 36, 152.
14. Ibid.

sions.[15] Although Luther was open to the possibility of women ministering in emergencies or when no men were available, his underlying assumption was that men were more suited to leadership and that they would do a better job. He saw this as their God-ordained role.[16] We see instances of this same thinking in today's churches, most frequently in regard to foreign missions. On the mission field women have taken leadership responsibilities they would never be assigned in their home churches. The rationale?— there were no men available on the field.

Luther allowed women to preach, baptize, and hear confessions in emergency situations, but basically saw them as less able leaders then men. Down through the years, other theologians have agreed. For instance, Fairbairn saw women as inherently unsuited for leadership because they lacked the necessary discernment, shrewdness, independence, and good judgment. He feared women would be unable to rise above "first impressions and outside appearances, to resist solicitations, and amid subtle entanglements and fierce conflicts to cleave unswervingly to the right."[17] While Fairbairn bases female limitations on their constitution and nature, Liddon believes that, among other things, the need to silence women is based on their tendency to be misled. The fact that she was deceived by Satan merely confirms "the experience of all ages that woman is *more easily* led away than man."[18] Few would say that out loud today. But one wonders if the notion still prevails, silently undermining women's leadership and challenging their right to minister in positions of authority.

15. Luther, *Works,* vol. 32, 50

16. Luther, *Works,* vol. 36, 151.

17. Fairbairn, *Pastoral Epistles,* 129.

18. Liddon, *Timothy,* 19. Italics in the quote are Liddon's.

FEMININE ATTITUDE

Years ago I read one of those books meant to help women be women. It warned women against doing *masculine* chores. Wives should not do anything that would threaten their husband's masculinity. But if it were unavoidable to take on a masculine task, she should do so in a feminine manner, in a way that demonstrated her female helplessness. For instance, if her husband wasn't around and she needed to hang a picture, she could pound a nail into the wall herself, but she should only do so in a feminine manner. At this point my imagination short-circuited and I could only conclude— and I sincerely trust this is not what the author intended—that she should only pound a nail in the wall if she made sure it was crooked.

I am the first to acknowledge that men and women are different and I am all for men being masculine and women being feminine, even though I'm not always sure what that means. But I am opposed to women not doing things well, fearing that if they are too strong, too assertive, or too capable they will lose their femininity. Sometimes it is a fine line. And down through the years, theologians have shared ideas about what is and what is not appropriate behavior for women.

In response to the question of whether all women are subject to all men or if only wives are subject to their husbands John Calvin said, "On this account all women are born, that they may acknowledge themselves inferior in consequence of the superiority of the male sex."[19] He understood men's superiority over women as God-given and that women should not balk at it. "Let the woman be satisfied with her state of subjection, and not take it amiss that she is made inferior to the more distinguished sex."[20] Calvin suggested that the appropriate role for women was to resign themselves to their inferior status. Things were what they were.

19. Calvin, *Corinthians*, 358.
20. Calvin, *Corinthians*, 361.

Matthew Henry also believed women were in a subordinate position. He said, "This is the situation in which God has placed her; and for that reason she should have a mind suited to her rank, and not do any thing that looks like an affectation of changing places."[21] He believed that women held an inferior God-given rank and were expected to be content within their limited sphere. I think I know what he is trying to say, but it is a short step from maintaining a mind suited to an inferior rank and giving up on ever trying to do anything . . . well, anything superior.

Hildegard of Bingen (1098–1179) was a medieval mystic who wrote music, poetry, and books. In addition, she established at least two convents and traveled widely preaching to a variety of audiences.[22] Because of her many accomplishments, it is interesting what she understood God saying to her about the ministry of women in regard to the priesthood. "So too those of female sex should not approach the office of My altar; for they are an infirm and weak habitation, appointed to bear children and diligently nurture them."[23] She elaborates by describing how women cannot conceive children by themselves but through men, "as the ground is plowed not by itself but by a farmer."[24] She goes on to say that women must not be in the priesthood, but can "sing the praise of her Creator, as the earth can receive rain to water its fruits."[25] These passive images of the ground accepting the plow and receiving the rain may be the result of her personal spiritual experience in regard to the visions she received, or it could be a reflection of the culture of her time. At any rate, she is an interesting example of a medieval woman with an active ministry walking a tightrope between influential ministry and what she believed were God-given limitations.

21. M. Henry, *Commentary,* 561.

22. Newman, *Scivias,* 9–10. See also Furlong, *Visions and Longings,* 84–86.

23. Hildegard of Bingen, *Scivias,* 2.76.

24. Ibid.

25. Ibid.

Even today there are women who travel the globe urging other women to stay home and take care of their families as God intended. This is as ironic as Hildegard saying that women were "appointed to bear children and diligently nurture them," while she carried on as a strong leader, traveling the countryside preaching and establishing convents. We sometimes cling to an idea—even preach it—while living out something quite different. Does this mean that we are compromising God's ideal, not walking our talk? Or does it mean we are mouthing the party line on the one hand and living out our true calling on the other? I don't think it's always easy to know. But I think the question is one we must ask ourselves.

Albert Barnes (1798–1870) had opinions about how women should behave. "Their station in life demands modesty, humility, and they should be free from the ostentation of appearing so much in public as to take part in the public services of teaching and praying."[26] He says that public ministry does not suit the rank of women and that God "appointed *men* to rule; to hold offices; to instruct and govern the church; and it is improper that women should assume that office upon themselves."[27]

Barnes and a number of other early theologians did not hesitate to lay out expectations and behavioral guidelines for women, guidelines that matched their perceptions of women as modest, somewhat helpless individuals who should understand their inferior rank and act accordingly.

OPPORTUNITIES AND LIMITATION

In New Testament times, the marketplace and public spheres were male domains while private households were female realms.[28] Since it was common for the early church to meet in private homes (Acts 2:46; Rom 16:5; Col 4:15; Phlm 2), it may have been accept-

---

26. Barnes, *New Testament,* 275

27. Ibid. Italics in the quote are Barnes's.

28. Torjesen, *Women Priests,* 59.

able for women to be involved with the ministries going on in their households.[29] Paul mentions a number of women—women such as Priscilla, Tryphena, Tryphosa, Mary, Junia, and Phoebe—who were heavily involved in the New Testament church. Later, however, as the church became more central to society and services became public, the role of women changed.[30] Although they were still involved in ministry, they were restricted from public leadership and were not allowed to become priests.

Chrysostom, was an early theologian (347–407), who held interesting views regarding women in ministry. In *On the Priesthood*, he addresses difficulties faced by immature and inexperienced priests, including the problem of becoming enmeshed with and manipulated by domineering women. Although women were excluded from formal leadership, he observed that they "forcibly push themselves in, and, since they can do nothing personally, they do everything by proxy."[31] Apparently women in his day—with no recognized leadership positions in the church—were managing to rebuke and bitterly criticize church leaders, driving objectionable men from the priesthood, while ensuring that their favorites were appointed to prestigious positions.[32] Chrysostom's concern here was with ineffectual and incompetent priests and he sees pushy and manipulative women as part of the problem.

Although Chrysostom believed women were restricted from teaching in public, he recognized that they could teach children, instruct their unbelieving husbands and, as Priscilla did, instruct men in private. "When she is wiser, then he [Paul] does not forbid her teaching and improving him."[33] He describes the women in Paul's day in glowing terms and recognized their involvement in ministry. "For the women of those days were more spirited than

29. Ibid., 82.
30. Ibid., 157.
31. Chrysostom, *Priesthood*, 78.
32. Ibid.
33. Chrysostom, "Romans," 554.

lions, sharing with the Apostles their labors for the Gospel's sake. In this way they went traveling with them, and also performed all other ministries."[34] He assumes Junia, mentioned in Romans 16:7 is a woman and an apostle. He marvels at her devotion, a devotion so great she was "counted worthy of the appellation of apostle!"[35] Chrysostom was critical of aggressive manipulative women, but had high respect for women when they were godly and wise and he recognized them as important church leaders.

Although women were banned from the priesthood, during the Middle Ages many women held important leadership positions in convents and monasteries. A number of female mystics were active during this time period, including Heloise (1100–63), Clare of Assisi (1196–1263), Catherine of Siena (1347–80), Margery Kempe (1373–1439), and Julian of Norwich (1342–1416).[36] These women were recognized for their spiritual leadership, depth, and insight and many of their writings are still in print today.

The Protestant Reformation broke through many of the barriers between clergy and laity. But it did not usher in widespread ministry opportunities for women. In fact, with the advent of Protestantism, the convents and monasteries were under attack and some of the leadership opportunities they had provided for women were abolished.[37] Nevertheless, women were often influential and a few of them earned the esteem of theologians and church leaders. Some of them, such as Katherine von Bora Luther and Katherine Zell, were active in the revolt against the Catholic Church and worked alongside their preacher husbands to promote the purposes of the Protestant Reformation. Women as well as men got caught up in the brutality that marked the interactions between Catholics and Protestants during the Reformation, and

34. Ibid.

35. Chrysostom, "Romans," 554–55

36. Furlong gives brief biographies of these medieval women, along with several others, 47–249.

37. Tucker and Liefeld. *Daughters*, 198–99.

a number of women were persecuted, tortured, and even burned at the stake. Some women who did not leave Catholicism, such as Charitas Pirckheimer, Teresa of Avila, and Jacoba Bartolini, were, nevertheless, influential as part of the reformation of the Catholic Church.[38]

Although the limitations on women's formal leadership in the church continued in the years following the Reformation, a number of exceptional women were influential in the church and in society. Mary Penington, Sor Juana Ines de la Cruz, Madame Jeanne Guyon, Anne Hutchinson, Sarah Edwards, and Susanna Wesley[39] ministered in various ways during the 1600s and 1700s. Although not holding public offices of leadership, some of these women ministered in the midst of great controversy.

A century later, Charles Hodge (1797–1878), commenting on 1 Corinthians 11:5, acknowledged that women were allowed to prophecy, but insisted that they could only do so in private.[40] He based this rule of public silence on the *rational* ground that women are to be in a "relation of subordination" and on the *scriptural* ground that according to both the Old and New Testaments "the doctrine that women should be in subjection is clearly revealed."[41] An interesting side note is Hodge's broad understanding of what it means to prophesy. "The prophets of God, therefore, were his spokesmen, into whose mouth the Lord put the words which they were to utter to the people. To *prophesy*, in Scripture, is accordingly, to speak under divine inspiration; not merely to predict future events, but to deliver, as the organ of the Holy Ghost, the messages of God to men, whether in the form of doctrine, exhortation, consolation, or prediction"[42] Hodge's description of prophesying sounds very much like preaching. This is in contrast to House,

38. Tucker and Liefield, *Daughters,* 178–206
39. Tucker and Liefeld, *Daughters,* 210, 212–16, 220–24, 234, 236–38.
40. Hodge, *Corinthians,* 304–5.
41. Ibid.
42. Ibid., 207

who, as we saw earlier makes a finer distinction between prophesying and preaching God's Word, and concludes that it is OK for women to prophesy, but they should not be allowed to preach or teach.[43]

During the nineteenth century the mainline churches remained closed to women in leadership, particularly in regard to ordination. However, other opportunities for ministry opened up. Prominent theologians such as Jonathan Edwards, John Wesley, and A.B. Simpson[44] were supportive of women in ministry and enlisted their help. Catherine Booth, Phoebe Palmer, Amanda Smith, and Hannah Whitall Smith were active in evangelism, preaching, and writing; Frances Willard and Carry Nation were involved in social work and the temperance movement; Antoinette Brown was the first woman to receive full ministerial ordination; and Anne Hasseltine Judson, Maria Taylor, and Amy Carmichael distinguished themselves in missionary work.[45] It was during this time period that Mary Baker Eddy and Ellen G. White started large, cultish religious movements.[46] While we would consider these negative examples, they illustrate that women were able to have wide influence during this time period. Many women—though still often banned from ordination and the more formal church offices—enlisted to serve in the great evangelistic, social, and missionary efforts of the nineteenth century and had a profound and positive influence.

INTERDEPENDENCY

In a later chapter I will spend time exploring the head and body metaphor Paul used frequently. It is a powerful image of interdependency. Getting a fresh understanding of Paul's head and body

43. House, *Role of Women in Ministry*, 112–24.
44. Tucker and Liefeld, *Daughters,* 240, 287
45. Ibid., 207–327.
46. Ibid., 276–77.

metaphor has cleared up much of my confusion about God's view of women. And in my research I found a few theologians who verbalized the interdependency implied in this image. While I don't think they fully grasped Paul's meaning, they glimpsed what he was getting at.

Chrysostom is one of the early theologians who recognized this interdependency. "The wife is a second authority; let not her then demand equality, for she is under the head; nor let him despise her as being in subjection, for she is the body; and if the head despises the body, it will itself also perish."[47] The head and body metaphor is a powerful one and at least to some extent Chrysostom understood that the head could not survive without the body. Although Chrysostom assumed that women did not have the same authority and status as men, he nevertheless acknowledged they were critical to the survival of the human race.

Thomas Aquinas is credited with the statement about Adam's rib that is still frequently used to describe a balanced relationship between men and women and occasionally shows up in contemporary wedding ceremonies—"for the woman should neither use authority over man, and so she was not made from his head; nor was it right for her to be subject to man's contempt as his slave, so she was not made from his feet."[48] While assuming a male/female hierarchy, Aquinas recognizes that women should not be treated as servants.

As we saw earlier, John Calvin believed women were inferior to men in numerous ways. But he also recognized their interdependence and said that men and women should be joined together in goodwill. More than other theologians, he seemed to recognize the visceral connection between men and women described by Paul. "If they are separated, they are like the mutilated members of a mangled body. Let them, therefore, be connected with each other

---

47. Chrysostom, "Ephesians," 5:31ff.
48. Aquinas, *Basic Writings*, 882–83.

by the bond of mutual duty."[49] While his idea of *mutual duty* may be far removed from my idea of male/female equality, I believe he glimpsed what Paul was getting at in 1 Corinthians 11. I believe the *mangled body* image he has in mind is that of a headless carcass, or a head separated from its body—the powerful head and body metaphor Paul uses to illustrate interdependency between men and women, the Father and the Son, and Christ and the Church.

SUMMARY

In the current debate regarding the role of women, complementarians attempt to separate essence from function and make the case that women are equal in the essence of their beings, but have functional limitations in regard to ministry and leadership. As we have seen in this chapter, many early theologians did not distinguish between equality of essence and equality of function. They simply saw women as inferior beings. It should not surprise us that this pervasive attitude toward women down through the centuries still impacts us today.

Throughout history women have experienced both restrictions on their ministry and admiration for their achievements. This was true in early church history and continued on through the time of the Protestant Reformation. Although women became more involved in ministry following the Reformation, they still experienced limitations. This has been a consistent pattern in church history and is considered by some a demonstration of faithfulness to biblical principles[50] and by others as a sometimes necessary, but unfortunate, heritage that should be replaced by a "structure that utilizes all spiritual gifts."[51]

---

49. Calvin, *Corinthians,* 359–60.

50. Weinrich, "Women in the History," *279.*

51. Kimball, "Nature," 478.

Chrysostom's early frustration with pushy women who, restricted from church leadership, "do everything by proxy,"[52] raises an interesting possibility. Chrysostom's concern was for inexperienced and ineffectual priests who were being criticized and manipulated by strong, domineering women. The result was chaos. But what if women had not been banned from leadership? What if both able men and capable women had been carefully trained for leadership positions? What if ineffectual men had not been allowed into leadership positions they were not ready for and if resourceful women had not been sidelined and frustrated? Is it not possible that recognizing the leadership gifts—as well as the weaknesses—of both men and women would have proved to be a better system? That is the possibility that keeps me keeping on, that makes it difficult for me to put this issue to rest. Although I believe we have grown in our understanding of the value and worth of women, there are still faulty presuppositions and unexamined theological positions that need further exploration.

In this chapter and the two previous ones, we have been exploring how the church has viewed subordination in regard to relationships within the Trinity and between men and women. We have seen that down through the centuries, theologians were anxious to defend the equality of the Father and the Son. When it comes to the view of women, however, the story is different. A survey of church tradition indicates that contrary to complementarians who believe women are equal in essence, but subordinate in function, the historic view of the church was that women were inferior in both essence and function. Although, as we have seen, women have worked along side men in many ways and have had significant ministries, there is still a not-so-hidden assumption that women "have their place," and should not act otherwise. They should not act as equals.

Church history is important. The orthodox Christian view is important. Knowing what theologians have claimed down through

---

52. Chrysostom, *Priesthood*, 78.

the years is well and good. But what does the Bible say? That's what we will look at in the next chapter. How is it that Bible-believing Christians can come up with such different interpretations about the Trinity and about the role of women?

6

Bible: What Is the Message?

IT IS important to understand what the current controversy regarding the role of women is all about, and it is certainly helpful to know what the church has taught down through the centuries. But what about the Bible? What does the Bible say?

In this chapter exploring what the Bible says about equality and subordination, we will look at three major biblical themes. The first theme I will overview is the movement in scripture as access to God expands from the limitations imposed by the Israelite laws to the freedom proclaimed by the gospel of Christ. The second is the way that God frequently and surprisingly enlists the youngest, smallest, and weakest to carry out his work. The third is the consistent theme of compassion and justice.

In the next chapter we will get more specific regarding Paul's writings and a number of biblical passages interpreted differently by egalitarians and complementarians. But in this chapter we will look at the overall message of the Bible. Before I do that, however, I want to share something of my personal journey regarding biblical interpretation and application. My training has primarily been shaped by grammatical-historical exegesis with an early smattering of what I would call literalism. My grammatical-historical mindset keeps me aware that the context and the meaning of words are important for the correct interpretation of scripture. Literalism mainly comes down to me in half-remembered warnings about the dangers of abandoning the literal interpretation of biblical passages in favor of mythical, literary, or metaphysical approaches. Today I recognize that figures of speech must be taken into consideration. While there is some risk that literary devices can be used to explain away biblical truth, we do biblical interpretation no favor by ignoring the writing style or intention of the authors. Sarah Sumner speaks to this in her book, *Men and Women in the Church.* "Metaphors aren't meant to be taken literally, but neither are they meant to be ignored. It is wrong to disregard a biblical metaphor. It is wrong because the metaphors are inspired by God and therefore profitable as well as authoritative."[1] It is important to remember that recognizing literary devices for what they are does not undermine scripture, but instead provides a way to better understand what God is trying to tell us. We need to recognize when writers are using figures of speech or we will miss what the author is really trying to say.

We all bring our own background, circumstances, and perceptions with us when we read the Bible. I bring with me what I learned in Sunday school as a child, the sermons I've heard, books I've read, as well as my academic training. In addition, I read it as a woman. And while I read it as a woman, I have never divided it into segments, some meant for males and others for females. And the Bible is not divided in such a way that there are *Ten Commandments for Women*, *Female Spiritual Gifts*, or *Feminine Strategies for Evangelism.*

While it's true there are more examples and stories in the Bible about men than women, I don't assume the male examples are meaningless for me, as a woman. For instance, when I read the story about David going out to meet Goliath, I don't brush the story aside and wonder what the women are doing back in town. No, I understand the story is about courage and trusting God and that it is a story for all people. Likewise, Mary's great expression of faith at the annunciation is an example for men and women alike.

There are a few passages directed specifically toward men or women. For instance, in 1 Peter 3, Peter tells women to submit to their husbands and then tells men to be considerate of their wives.

1. Sumner, *Men and Women,* 117.

But even here, Peter soon turns his attention to all Christians, admonishing them to "always be prepared to give an answer" to those who asked about their hope (1 Pet 3:13). Even though a few verses earlier Peter instructed wives to be gentle and quiet, we can't assume women are supposed to whisper discreetly to one another about their hope while men are expected to be bold and aggressive. No, he is saying that all Christians—men and women alike—should be prepared to "proclaim their hope" and that both men and women should answer with "gentleness and respect" (1 Pet 3:16). The Bible is written for men and women alike and both are accountable to it. Even so, I cannot leave my womanhood aside when I read the Bible and I believe it is important to hear the perspectives of both men and women in order to hear the full message of scripture. To begin, let's look at the theme of freedom in Christ.

FREEDOM IN CHRIST

The Bible is God's revelation and record of his dealings with mankind. The fact that the Bible is divided into two Testaments—the Old and the New—bears witness to movement and change. God never changes, but down through the centuries he has accommodated himself to mankind in a variety of ways (Heb 1:12) and his expectations have changed as the redemption plan has unfolded. The Old Testament records God's perfect creation, man's fall into sin, the promise of a Messiah, the necessity of the law, and mankind's consistent failure to live up to God's standards. The New Testament records the coming of the Messiah in fulfillment of the Old Testament promise and the beginning of the Church. Imbedded in this history is movement—movement from limitations regarding who could approach God to freedom in Christ and the breaking down of those barriers (Heb 1:1–22; Eph 2:11–22).

In *All God's People,* John E. Phelan describes this forward movement as former losers become winners as old barriers "are left behind in the new thing God is doing."[2] Phelan points out that in Mark 5 Jesus touches the lives of three holiness "losers." First he heals the demon-possessed man who had four strikes against him—a Gentile, possessed by demons, living in a graveyard, and surrounded by pigs. Then Jesus crosses to the other side of the lake and heals the woman with a bleeding problem. Right after that, Jesus continued on his way to the home of Jairus, whose daughter had just died. Although touching the dead made you unclean, Jesus took her hand and she came back to life. Death, demons, swine, female blood, and Gentiles were all considered unclean in Jesus' day.

Jesus demonstrated an attitude toward holiness very different from the legalistic Jewish leaders. The Jewish leaders considered holiness fragile and avoided anything "unclean." But Jesus saw holiness as powerful. Jesus didn't believe it was necessary to separate and isolate in order to preserve and protect holiness.[3] He demonstrated that holiness is inner more than outer and that ultimately it is a God-given access to himself.

This access to God was dramatically demonstrated at the crucifixion. When Jesus died, the curtain that kept everyone except the high priest away from the Holy of Holies was ripped from top to bottom, a graphic illustration that now everyone had direct access to God (Mark 15:38).[4] Phelan says, "All God's people are priests. All God's people are holy. All God's people have the Spirit."[5] This expanded access to God is hinted at in Genesis (Gen 17:1–14), proclaimed by the prophets (Isa 56:3–7), and fulfilled in the life, death, and resurrection of Jesus (Heb 7:23–27).

Another author who stresses the importance of the overall message of scripture is Mary Stewart Van Leeuwen. In *Gender and Grace* Van Leeuwen looks to the entire scope of the Bible and the

2. Phelan, *God's People*, vii.

3. Ibid., 39.

4. Ibid., 41.

5. Ibid., 51.

direction in which God has been moving throughout the centuries. She specifically looks at what the Bible has to say about gender. "I have not assumed that the Bible is either silent or hopelessly ambiguous on this matter [male/female equality], but rather that it is an unfolding drama in which God's salvation is made available to more and more groups previously considered marginal."[6] She cites Galatians 3:28 as a reminder that the privileges and responsibilities of salvation and access to God now extend beyond Jewish males to Gentiles, slaves, and women.

Both Van Leeuwen and Phelan take the overall message of the Bible seriously and they both point out that the unfolding revelation regarding the accessibility of God and his salvation is not limited to people of a specific nationality, social strata, or gender. Strictly speaking, God has always been accessible to everyone. However, the social and religious structures that were once necessary have been done away with in the New Covenant (Gal 3:23–25).

God is calling unto himself a royal priesthood made up of all believers. Priesthood implies personal access to God as well as ministry to others. In looking at the overall message of the Bible, we need to consider the movement of scripture from the Old Testament to the New. The Bible as a whole records the movement from limitations on God's accessibility in the ancient past to the eventual embracing of all mankind. This embracing of all mankind was hinted at throughout scripture and fulfilled in Jesus.

Another overall biblical theme we need to consider is the fascinating way that God sovereignly and surprisingly chose younger, smaller, or weaker individuals to carry out his work. He uses strong and powerful people as well, but he often chooses to work through the powerless. Jesus underscores this theme when he says that the first shall be last and the last shall be first. Jesus confronted the legalistic Jewish system and redefined who is first.

6. Van Leeuwen, *Gender,* 234.

SOVEREIGN SURPRISES

One of the profound understandings I gained as a child in Sunday school was that God often went against the cultural grain when choosing whom he would use to carry out his purposes. He was full of sovereign surprises. This theme is evident in many Old Testament stories. When Isaac and Rebekah gave birth to twins, God was explicit in explaining who would have precedence. It wasn't going to be Esau, the oldest. "Two nations are in your womb, and two people from within you will be separated; one people will be stronger than the other, and the older will serve the younger" (Gen 25:23). This idea of the older serving the younger was totally at odds with the culture of the day. Nevertheless, a number of years later, God's intention was confirmed when Jacob usurped Esau's birthright, the blessing that would normally have been bestowed on the oldest son (Gen 27). God chose to work through the younger son.

In the book of Judges we find further examples. God sometimes chose the weak and powerless to deliver his people. God found Gideon hiding in a wine press and called him to lead the Israelites against the Midianites. Gideon hesitated. "'But Lord,' Gideon asked, 'how can I save Israel? My clan is the weakest in Manasseh, and I am the least in my family.'" God assured Gideon that he would be with him and that he would "strike down the Midianites as if they were but one man" (Judg 6:15–16). Clearly God was not concerned about the size of Gideon's clan or the status he held in his family.

A short time before that, God had used two women, Deborah and Jael, to deliver the Israelites from the Canaanites. Deborah had pleaded with Barak, the son of Abinoam, to lead the Israelite army into battle. But he refused, insisting that she go with him. Deborah, perhaps aware that this would violate cultural tradition is, nevertheless, confident that God would not hesitate to work in this unusual way. "'Very well,' Deborah said, 'I will go with you.

But because of the way you are going about this, the honor will not be yours, for the Lord will hand Sisera over to a woman'" (Judg 4:9). And that is exactly what happened. Deborah accompanied Barak to the battlefront, the Israelite army had a decisive victory against Sisera, and a woman named Jael killed Sisera in her tent. Two women helped bring down the Midianites.

There are other lives we could look at, such as Abel, Joseph, and David, but the above examples illustrate that in the Old Testament God did not hesitate to reverse the natural order and cultural norms to accomplish his purposes. When we get to the New Testament, the picture becomes even clearer.

In Jesus' words and actions we see this unusual approach again and again. He sidesteps the traditions of the religious and political leaders of his day and focuses his attention on those with hearts open to him (Matt 15:1–28); he shocks the disciples by conversing with a Samaritan woman (John 4:1–26); and he selects fishermen, tax collectors, and political zealots to be his closest companions (Matt 4:18–22; Luke 6:15; Matt 9:9). He is so at home with the low life that he is labeled a glutton and a drunkard (Luke 7:33–35). And to make sure we don't think he has simply stumbled into a careless lifestyle, Jesus points out the principle behind his actions. He is making a statement. "But many who are first will be last, and many who are last will be first" (Matt 19:30). God's perspective on things runs counter to culture, societal norms, and what we would consider the natural order of things.

In the face of such a consistent theme, it seems obvious that God is more interested in displaying his power than in relying on the strength of his followers or in conforming to cultural, social or religious patterns of privilege, status, and power. One of the consistent biblical themes is that in his sovereignty God frequently chooses the powerless, the humble, and the disenfranchised to carry out his purposes. Society does it one way. God does it another.

In addition to the overall theme of the Bible that takes us from limitations to freedom, and the repeated message that God sovereignly carries out his work in surprising ways, there is an additional theme stressing the importance of justice and compassion toward the oppressed and exploited.

COMPASSION AND JUSTICE

The message in the Bible regarding those who are poor and oppressed is consistent from beginning to end. In Exodus the Israelites were reminded to not mistreat or oppress aliens, take advantage of widows or orphans, pervert justice by ganging up on people, show favoritism, or deny justice to the poor (Exod 22:21—23:9). In Leviticus the Israelites were told to leave remnants of their crops behind so the poor and the alien could glean what was left (Lev 19:10; 23:22). In Deuteronomy they were warned against scheming to use their social system to take advantage of the poor (Deut. 15:7–11; 24:14–15). The prophet Micah pointed out that the Lord loved justice, mercy, and humility (Mic 6:8). There are other Old Testament reminders that justice is a high priority with God (Prov 21:3; Hos 6:6).

In the New Testament there are exhortations against favoritism (Luke 14:12–14; Gal 2:10), warnings about discriminating against Gentiles (Gal 3:28, 29; Rom 3:21–30; 1 Cor 10:31–33; Eph 3:6), and admonitions against rejecting the poor (Jas 2:1–5). Throughout the Bible there are numerous reprimands regarding partiality, prejudice, and injustice. But let's take a look at just one Old Testament story. Tucked away in the book of Numbers is an interesting tale about five women taking a stand against injustice.

The Israelites are on the plains of Moab along the river Jordan across from Jericho. Moses and Eleazar the priest had recently taken a census and allotted an inheritance of land to each clan. The census was all about men—the descendants of Reuben, Simeon and Manasseh . . . the clan of Perez, Jashub, and Shechem . . . men over twenty years of age . . . 601,730 men.

Then something unusual happens. Into this man's world walk five women—Mahlah, Noah, Hoglah, Milcah, and Tirzah. They are the daughters of Zelophehad. Zelophehad was a descendant of Manasseh, of the clan of Gilead. Zelophehad had no sons and his daughters were on a mission. They entered the Tent of Meeting and took their stand before the whole assembly, including Moses, Eleazar the priest, and the other leaders. They presented their case, reminding everyone that although their father had died in the desert, he was not a rebel. He had not joined together with Korah's followers against the Lord. "Why should our father's name disappear from his clan because he had no son? Give us property among our father's relatives" (Num 27:2–4).

The women are requesting to inherit land just like the men. If the women are nervous about making this request, it doesn't come across in their words, but they obviously remembered what had happened to Korah and his followers when they had overstepped their boundaries. Everyone remembered. Not too long before, God had nearly wiped out the line of Korah—the earth had opened up and fire had devoured 250 men. Why?—because they didn't know their place. They had rebelled against God. Wasn't that a powerful enough reminder to accept the status quo? What were these women thinking?

But when Moses brings the women's case before the Lord, God's response was probably not what the people expected. God said, "What Zelophehad's daughters are saying is right. You must certainly give them property as an inheritance among their father's relations and turn their father's inheritance over to them" (Num 27:5–7).

The people must have sighed in relief and muttered in confusion. Women could inherit just like men? What was God thinking? Because these five women had the courage to approach Moses and Eleazar, the inheritance policy was changed (Num 27:11). In contrast to the Kohathites who earlier had overstepped their boundaries in open rebellion, the daughters of Zelophehad presented their request in a firm but respectful manner. Can you imagine the courage it took those women to approach Moses in front of the whole assembly? Can you imagine how they must have felt when God said, "You know what, they're right"? What a moment that must have been.

Our daughter is a counselor at a school with a high percentage of at-risk kids. She has a bachelor's degree in social work and a master's degree in counseling. She understands the importance of confronting injustice and standing up for the oppressed. When she reminded me about this story, she said, "What if those women hadn't stepped forward and raised the issue?" What indeed? This little story in the book of Numbers, hidden away in a list of clans, forefathers, and male descendants, demonstrates there are times when it is important to stand up for justice, to question the status quo, and to seek redress.

As we have looked at the overall message of the Bible, we have seen there is movement leading from limited access to God under the Mosaic Law to freedom of access through Christ. We have also noticed that when God chose people to carry out His work He often overturned major cultural assumptions. Rather than choosing the oldest, the strongest, or the next in line, he often chose someone unexpected, someone with a submissive, humble heart through whom he could demonstrate his power. And finally, we have seen that in the Bible there are consistent themes of justice and compassion. God expects us to have mercy on the underdog, to be generous to those who are poor, and to rectify social or political systems that are unfair.

The Bible is not a hammer for men to use against women or for women to use against men. Instead it is a remarkable reminder to both men and women to treat each other with love and respect. God did not intend for the Bible to be read selectively. Women are not somehow relegated to a partial gospel. The great commission is addressed to both men and women. Both men and women have spiritual gifts; both men and women are exhorted to strive for unity; both men and women are challenged to live lives worthy of their calling; and both men and women are called to live holy lives. And when Peter writes about the "priesthood of all believers," there is not a clause in small print excluding women from the *real* priesthood of all believers. The biblical themes of love, respect, justice, mercy, submission, and sacrifice apply to all Christians, men and women alike.

In later chapters we will elaborate on how these overall biblical themes have relevance regarding the role of women. But in the next chapter we narrow our focus and look at the purpose of Paul's ministry and explore some of the more controversial biblical passages regarding women.

7

Bible: Who Interprets It?

T HERE ARE those who claim that the Bible says what it says and
there is only one right way to interpret it. While it may be true
there is only one right way to interpret it, it is not clear to me who
gets to decide what that right way is. For it is obvious that not everyone interprets it the same. At the core of the current debate among
evangelical theologians regarding the role of women is the question
of how to interpret scripture. As we saw in chapter 2, egalitarians
and complementarians can look at the same passages and come up
with entirely different conclusions. One of the biggest hurdles for
egalitarians is determining how to deal with scripture passages that
seem to clearly and explicitly speak to the subordinate role of women
(I Tim 2:11–15; 1 Cor 11:1–16; 1 Cor 14:33b–38). A big challenge
for complementarians is dealing with the passages that stress the
priesthood of all believers, unity, giftedness, and oneness in Christ
(1 Pet 2:5, 9; John 17:20–23; Gal 3:28–29).

In this chapter we will explore how various passages regarding women and the Trinity are interpreted and draw some conclusions about their validity. Much disagreement and confusion
regarding the role of women is rooted in Paul's writings. Because
of this, and to better understand Paul's attitude toward women in
ministry, I will explore what the Bible says about the purpose of
Paul's ministry and the methods he used to illustrate his points.
After that we will look at biblical passages and concepts regarding
women in ministry, headship, and the Trinity.

PAUL'S PURPOSE AND METHODS

Paul was clear that the purpose of his ministry was to spread the gospel of Jesus Christ to all people (Rom 1:14). Although he sensed a responsibility toward everyone, he felt a special call to minister the gospel of Jesus Christ to the Gentiles (Rom 15:16, Gal 1:15) and he claimed that the message he had for the Gentiles was a mystery that had not been revealed to previous generations (Eph 3:4–6, Col 1:24–26). So how does a man entrusted with a special revelation from God for a people formerly perceived as outsiders go about sharing the good news?

Paul and other New Testament writers used every legitimate means at their disposal to share the gospel. They tried to ensure that the gospel was not unnecessarily offensive to the culture they were trying to reach (Acts 16:2) and they used Old Testament scripture (Rom 15:1–4), oral traditions (2 Tim 3:8),[1] non-canonical literature (Jude 14–15),[2] and the hermeneutical methods customary during the time in which they lived (Gal 3:16) to get the message across.

To begin, let's look at how they used Old Testament scripture. A casual reading of the New Testament may cause us to ask how we are to understand the ways in which Paul and other New Testament writers used the Old Testament to illustrate and stress the Christ event. Did they adhere to the grammatical-historical standards of today's evangelical theologians?

In *Inspiration and Incarnation*, Peter Enns takes a close look at the world in which the New Testament writers lived and the interpretive methods they used in their writings. "The odd uses of the Old Testament by New Testament authors are such a common dimension of the New Testament that it quickly becomes special pleading to argue otherwise." [3] Enns goes on to explain the Second Temple hermeneutical tradition, the hermeneutical approach

---

1. Wiersbe, *Commentary*, 2 Tim. 3:8.
2. Wiersbe, *Commentary*, Jude 14–15.
3. Enns, *Inspiration*, 116.

common during New Testament times. Writers following the Second Temple hermeneutical approach were as concerned with the hidden *true* meaning of the text as they were with the original context. Whether or not we agree with all of Enns's conclusions, he addresses an important question.

What *are* we to make of the way Paul and other New Testament writers use Old Testament scripture? For example, in Matthew's account of Joseph's dream warning him that Herod planned to kill Jesus, Matthew quotes Hosea 11:1: "So he got up, took the child and his mother during the night and left for Egypt, where he stayed until the death of Herod. And so was fulfilled what the Lord had said through the prophet: '*Out of Egypt I called my son*'" (Matt 2:14–15). In its original context the passage in Hosea is talking about God's deliverance of the Israelites from their slavery in Egypt. Matthew recognizes in it a reference to the deliverance of the child Jesus from King Herod and includes it in the advent story.

A cursory reading of these passages could lead one to assume the writers are improperly lifting the verses out of context. But let's take a deeper look at one example in Paul's writing—his use of the word "seed" in Galatians 3:16. Paul says, "The promises were spoken to Abraham and to his seed. The scripture does not say 'and to seeds,' meaning many people, but 'and to your seed,' meaning one person, who is Christ." Maxie D. Dunnam points out that "Paul surely knew that neither the Greek nor Hebrew plural of the word in question would have created a different meaning."[4] So, what is going on here?

---

4. Dunnam, *Commentary,* 70–71. See also Keener, *IVP Commentary,* Gal. 3:15–16, who sees Paul arguing his case "the way the rabbis often did," and Enns, *Inspiration,* on page 137–38. Theologians, such as Walvoord and Zuck, do not see Paul taking license or going overboard in the way he uses *seed* in Gal. 3:15–16. Instead they maintain that "The stress on seed (cf. Gen. 12:7; 13:15; 24:7), not seeds, was made simply to remind the readers that the faithful in Israel had always recognized that blessing would ultimately come through a single individual, the Messiah (cf. Gal. 3:19). Walvoord and Zuck, *Bible Knowledge Commentary,* Gal. 3:15–16.

I think the first thing going on is that in the original Old Testament context God is promising Abraham numerous offspring—as many as the stars in the sky and the sands of the sea (Gen 12:7; 13:14–16; 22:17; 32:12). However, along with this promise to Abraham is another promise—a Messianic promise (Gen 3:15; 18:18; 22:18)—which is fulfilled in the Christ event. But what interests me the most is the way Paul uses this passage to make his point about redemption for the Gentiles (Gal 3:14). I believe Paul's insistence that the passage does not say "'and to seeds,' meaning many people," when the obvious original context means exactly that, is an example of Paul using the interpretive method acceptable in the time in which he lived. Instead of acknowledging the original context *as well as* the Messianic promise, Paul says that it doesn't say "that," it says "this." He goes overboard. This is not an oversight on Paul's part, or a misunderstanding of Hebrew or Greek. It is instead a culturally appropriate argument based on the Old Testament Messianic promises. This is one example of the methods Paul used to illustrate his message.

Paul was committed to doing everything within his power to share the gospel. For the sake of the gospel—and for him the gospel included freedom from circumcision for the Gentiles—He was willing to be arrested, whipped, and imprisoned. Again and again he railed on certain Jews for insisting that Gentiles needed to be circumcised in order to be Christ followers (Gal 2:11–16; 6:12–16; Titus 1:10–11). At the same time, when he and Timothy were beginning a ministry near Timothy's home town, where there were many Jews who knew Timothy was Greek, he circumcised Timothy in order not to offend them (Acts 16:3). Why would Paul do something so inconsistent with what he preached?—something to which he was directly opposed? It is because he was determined to not let anything stand in the way of the spread of the gospel (1 Cor 9:20). We can see this same attitude in regard to eating meat, drinking wine, observing sacred days, going to court against a brother, and eating in an idol's temple (1 Cor. 6:6; 8:1–13; 10:31–33).

Paul was totally committed to sharing the gospel—especially to the Gentiles. (1 Cor 9: 21–23)—and went to extraordinary lengths to avoid offending others in regard to personal habits, religious practices, public behavior, or individual freedom. It is important for us to understand his purpose and the methods he used.

Next we will look at what the Bible says about women in ministry. Much of the controversy regarding the role of women is related to Paul's instructions in the epistles about their role—or non-role—in church ministry.

WOMEN IN MINISTRY

Paul's instructions that in the church "women are not allowed to speak" (1 Cor 14:4), or to teach (1 Tim 2:12), and "must be silent" (1 Tim 2:11), coupled with his mandate that elders are to be "the husband of one wife" (1 Tim 3:20) suggest significant biblical limitations regarding the ministry of women in the church.

It is a challenge to understand these passages in light of other passages which include women in the early stages of church development (Acts 1:14, Acts 8:3), in which Paul commends women such as Apphia, Chloe, Nympha, Priscilla, Phoebe, Mary, Tryphena, Persis, Julia, and Junia for their participation in his ministry (Phil 2, 1 Cor 1:11, Col 4:15, Rom 16:1–5), and in which Paul assumes that women will pray and prophesy in the church (1 Cor 11:4,5). Both the limitations Paul suggested, as well as the inclusion of women in early church ministry, must be considered to get an accurate biblical understanding of the role of women in ministry.

Complementarians cull deep theological implications regarding the role of women from 1 Corinthians 11:3–16 and 1 Timothy 2:11 while brushing aside other aspects of the passages. They easily dismiss the wearing of head coverings as cultural,[5] hesitate to say

5. Grudem, *Systematic Theology*, 333–34.

that women are more easily deceived than men,[6] and recognize that Paul could not have meant that women remain *completely* silent.[7] Nevertheless, they are able to find in these passages an order of creation mandate that defines masculinity and femininity and that cross-culturally justifies the functional subordination of women in the church and in the home for all time.[8]

It is difficult for me to believe that these two biblical references, both of which are fraught with complex interpretive difficulties, can sustain the weight of the *order of creation* implications heaped upon them. I believe Paul's references to creation order in 1 Corinthians and 1 Timothy 2 are for illustrative purposes and do not necessarily have implications regarding women's role in churches today. Paul is a persuasive writer and is intent on getting his message across. The creation account does not specify a subordinate role for women, and Paul himself backs away from such an interpretation in 1 Corinthian 11:11–12 when he points out that everything comes from God and that men and women are not independent of one another. He balances out his argument about head coverings by underscoring the mutuality and interdependence of men and women.

In these passages Paul is not endorsing a permanent subordinate role for women. Instead he is concerned about orderly worship and was trying to bring his points home to the Corinthians and Ephesians with illustrations he knew would make sense to them. Writers such as Piper and Grudem disregard such a possibility. "We do not think that it honors the integrity of Paul or the inspiration of scripture to claim that Paul resorted to arguing that his exhortations were rooted in the very order of creation and in

6. Moo, "What Does It Mean?" 190.

7. House, *Role of Women in Ministry*, 46.

8. Piper, "Biblical Complementarity, 51; Piper and Grudem, "Overview of Central Concerns," 64, 74.

the work of Christ in order to justify his sanctioning temporary accommodations to his culture."[9]

While Piper and Grudem insist that Paul would only base his arguments on creation if they had "abiding validity,"[10] I don't believe that is necessarily the case. In addition to the order of creation argument in the 1 Corinthians 11 passage, Paul puts forth an argument based on the *nature of things*. "Does not the very nature of things teach you that if a man has long hair, it is a disgrace to him, but that if a woman has long hair, it is her glory? For long hair is given to her as a covering" (11:14–15).

The very nature of things? My initial reaction to these verses was to wonder if men are unable to grow their hair as long as women. That doesn't seem to be the case. But then what does Paul mean by "the nature of things?" It sounds like an inbred reality. But John Calvin explains it as a cultural issue, not a natural, God-given *covering*. "He again set forth *nature* as mistress of decorum, and what was at that time in common use by universal consent and custom—even among the Greeks—he speaks of as being *natural*, for it was not always reckoned a disgrace for men to have long hair."[11] According to Calvin, what Paul refers to as *nature*, was in reality merely a custom of the time in which he lived. "Nay . . . in Greece it was reckoned an unbecoming thing for a man to allow his hair to grow long, so that those who did so were remarked as effeminate, he reckons as *nature* a custom that had come to be confirmed."[12]

When Paul suggests that the "very nature of things" teaches that it is a glory for women to have long hair, but disgraceful for men, his words have more weight than if he had just said it was customary for women to have long hair and men to have short hair. Paul argues that his exhortations regarding head coverings

9. Ibid., 67.
10. Ibid.
11. Calvin, *Corinthians*, 361–62.
12. Ibid.

are rooted in the very nature of things when in reality they are rooted in local custom.

In chapter 5 we established that in his writings Paul used metaphors, plays on words, Old Testament scripture, oral traditions, non-canonical literature, and the hermeneutical methods customary during his day to get his points across. I don't believe it is out of the question that, when appealing to the Corinthians regarding orderly worship and when writing to Timothy about protecting sound doctrine, he would appeal to the order of creation to make a point in a way that would get the attention of his readers and make sense to the people he was attempting to influence.[13] Just two chapters earlier, Paul told the Corinthians that he had "become all things to all men so that by all possible means" he might save some.[14] I think it is possible he would drive his points home with as much power as possible without intending to place limits on half the human race for all time. It doesn't disparage Paul's character or undermine the inspiration of scripture to understand Paul's words in 1 Corinthians 11 and 1 Timothy 2 as examples of Paul pulling out all the stops in order to make a point. Instead, it is a reasonable explanation for two passages of scripture that are otherwise difficult to interpret in light of Paul's other writings.

In the next section we will look at *headship*. As we have noted throughout this book, the word *head*, and the term *headship*, play significant and controversial roles in the way theologians interpret the relationship between men and women and between the Father and the Son. That is the issue we will look at next.

13. I agree with Giles when he says, "It would seem that in this passage [1 Cor. 11:3ff] Paul marshals a number of ad hominem arguments that would appeal directly to his readers to enforce a local cultural practice." Giles, *Trinity*, 178.

14. 1 Corinthians 9:22.

HEADSHIP

In its most apparent and basic meaning, the word *head* refers to the head of a body—the physical head of a physical body (Matt 8:20; Luke 12:7; John 19:30; Rev 19:12). In a number of passages, *head* refers to a cornerstone—the head of a corner. Specifically, Jesus is described as the cornerstone the builder rejected (Matt 21:42; Mark 12:10; Luke 20:17; 1 Pet 2:7). In a passage dealing with head coverings, relationships, and worship, Paul uses the term *head* metaphorically to illustrate interdependency. He describes Christ as the head of man, man the head of woman, and God the head of Christ (1 Cor 11:3). In a number of passages, Paul also uses a body and head metaphor to describe the interdependency of husbands and wives and of Christ and the Church (Eph 5:23; 1:22–23; 4:15–16; Col 1:18). In still other passages, Paul describes Christ as head over every power and authority (Col 2:9, Eph 1:22–23).

Complementarians generally argue that head means authority, while a number of egalitarians believe it means source. Some use a combination of the two. Sarah Sumner, in her book *Men and Women in the Church*, takes a somewhat different view. What was interesting to Sumner, and has been fascinating to me as well, is that for the most part extrabiblical sources use the word head in the same way it is used in the vast majority of New Testament references—as the physical head of a physical body.[15] In my own research, I had brushed that reality aside as both obvious and irrelevant. But I have come to believe that the more common way the word *head* is used in both the Bible and in extrabiblical sources may be the key to understanding Paul's use of the word as an image, part of a head and body metaphor.

A cursory look at the epistles reveals that for Paul the relationship between the head, the body, and the various parts of the body created a powerful image—an image illustrating interdependency. In the context of Corinthians alone, Paul uses this image a number

---

15. Sumner, *Men and Women*, 151.

of times. He tells the Corinthians that their bodies are "members of Christ himself" (1 Cor 6:15) and the "temple of the Holy Spirit" (1 Cor 6:19). He doesn't want them to forget that they are "all baptized by one Spirit into one body" (1 Cor 12:12). Using the body illustration to explain spiritual gifts, he says, "And the head cannot say to the feet, 'I don't need you!'" (1 Cor 12:21), and he concludes this section by reminding them that "you are the body of Christ, and each one of you is a part of it" (1 Cor 12:27). In all of these references, Paul is stressing the unity and interrelatedness of the parts of the body or of the head and the body. I believe that is what Paul is getting at in 1 Corinthians 11:3. The same thing is true for Ephesians 5, where Paul talks about man being the head of woman and Christ the head of the church, *his body.* He uses the head and body metaphor to illustrate relatedness and interdependency.

Of course, that is not the only way the word head is used in the New Testament. In Ephesians 1:22, Paul talks about Christ's reign "far above all rule and authority, power and dominion" and describes Christ as "the head over everything." In 1 Peter 2:7, Peter describes Christ as the cornerstone, or the "head of the corner." These passages suggest authority and/or importance. But I think Paul most frequently uses the word head—especially in the passages relevant to this study—as part of a head and body metaphor. And he uses it in a way that suggests interdependency not a hierarchical authority pattern. Paul recognizes how much we need each other and reminds us to be respectful and sensitive to one another and aware how our behavior and demeanor impact others.

In addition to the head and body metaphor, we need to give careful attention to the term *headship.* When we hear the term headship in regard to the relationship between men and women it is usually connected to 1 Corinthians 11:3 or Ephesians 5:23, passages in which Paul describes man as the head of woman. The term headship is used frequently in both egalitarian and complementarian literature. For instance in a section regarding the order of creation, Piper and Grudem talk about the "loving headship of husbands"[16] and Scanzoni and Hardesty question the "subjection of the wife and the headship of the husband."[17] Grudem talks about "biblical male headship"[18] and Knight says the "headship of the husband is established by God."[19] Grenz and Kjesbo talk about a "headship theology" that reserves senior pastor positions for men[20] and Giles refers to "conservative evangelicals who want to maintain the traditional pattern of male 'headship.'"[21]

This emphasis on *headship* is interesting because, although the word *head* is commonly used in the Bible, the term *headship* is not. In fact, the word headship, meaning a "position or office of head, chief, principal, or supreme governor,"[22] did not come into use until 1582 . . . A.D. So when Piper, Grudem, Scanzoni, Hardesty, Knight, Grenz, and Kjesbo talk about male "headship" it is important to recognize that they are interpreting, or acknowledging that others are interpreting, the word *head* in a way that suggests authority or leadership rather than interdependency. Assuming that the word head in 1 Corinthians 11:3 and Ephesians 5:23 indicates *headship* is not a straightforward reading of the passages. Instead, it is an interpretation.

When the term *headship*, a word that has specific meaning for us today, is read back into Paul's writings, Paul's powerful head and body metaphor becomes laden with bureaucracy. It has become a –*ship*, a rank or office. This take-over of Paul's profound metaphor has two unfortunate results. First, it weighs it down with connotations that go beyond Paul's original intention, and second, it sucks

16. Piper and Grudem, "Overview of Central Concerns," 73–74.

17. Scanzoni and Hardesty, *Meant to Be*, 98.

18. Grudem, *Evangelical Feminism*, 492.

19. Knight, "Husbands and Wives," 174.

20. Grenz and Kjesbo, *Women in the Church,* 33.

21. Giles, *Trinity*, 16.

22. Dictionary.com Unabridged (v 1.1).

the life from it. Instead of describing an interdependent head and body relationship, Paul's profound metaphor is turned into a static state of being and the original meaning is distorted.

Sarah Sumner describes the relief she felt when she realized Paul used the head and body metaphor to help the Corinthians to *see*—rather than intellectually comprehend—what he was saying about relationships. "It relieved me to find out that we are not responsible to mentally compute exactly what it means for Christ to be the head of every man, and for the man to be head of a woman, and for God to be the head of Christ."[23] According to Sumner, Paul wanted the Corinthians to see these relationships as a picture rather than as a three-point outline.

In the course of this study I have come to see this head and body metaphor in the way Sumner describes. It has gone from words on a page to a vivid image. Calvin describes the separation of men and women as the "mutilated members of a mangled body."[24] Which is more gruesome, a head with no body or a body with no head? I don't think we can say. Both are hideous.

In my high school English class, we read a story about four teenagers recklessly speeding around the countryside in a convertible. On a dark country road they crashed into a drawbridge that was in the process of opening up for a boat to go through. When the ambulance arrived they found four decapitated bodies in the wrecked convertible. Which is more gruesome?—to imagine those four bodies strapped into seatbelts with no heads or to imagine the heads of four teenagers floating down the river separated from their bodies? We can't say. We just recognize it is an ugly, unnatural distortion of the way things are supposed to be.

I don't think that when Paul talks about man as the head of woman, or God as the head of Christ, we can assume he is referring to a relationship that is hierarchical and based on one person having authority over another. Instead, I believe he is using the terms

23. Sumner, *Men and Women*, 183.

24. Calvin, *Corinthians*, 359–60.

in much the way as he does throughout the book of Corinthians, as a metaphor for unity and interdependency. The last set of passages we will look at in this chapter are those dealing with the Trinity.

THE TRINITY

Although the term Trinity is not in the Bible, the doctrine of the Trinity is foundational to the Christian faith. So, upon what are the doctrine of the Trinity and the deity of Jesus Christ based? One of the most important passages in the Bible about the deity of Christ is Philippians 2:5–11. It describes Jesus—in his very nature God—humbling himself, taking on the nature of man, being obedient unto death, and then being raised back to authority and power. Encapsulated within these few verses are Jesus' deity, incarnation, and ultimate return to exaltation and authority. In other passages we learn that Jesus came from the Father (John 1:14); that he is the way to the Father (John 14:6); that he is one with the Father (John 10:30); and that his essence, purpose, and works are the same as the Father's (John 1:1; 5:21; 10:30; 14:9–11).

Jesus' humanity, his deity, and his oneness with the Father form a mystery we are unable to fully explain. In his humanity, Jesus' knowledge appears to be limited. During his life on earth, Jesus submitted, prayed, learned obedience, and grew in wisdom (Heb 5:7–10; Luke 2:40; Mark 13:32). He came down from heaven to do the will of the Father and did nothing on his own authority, but spoke as the Father taught him (John 6:38, 8:20). Although Christ came to earth and went to the cross in obedience to the Father (Matt 26:36–45; Mark 14:32–41; Luke 22:39–46), he at the same time voluntarily laid down his own life (John 10:18). Christ is the fullness of God in bodily form and head over every power and authority (Col 2:9). Christ is the power and wisdom of God. God is all in all and Christ is God over all, forever to be praised (1 Cor 1:24, 15:20–28; Rom. 9:5).

In these verses we see Jesus' subordination during the incarnation as well as his eternal equality and deity. Clarification that the Son's subordination is limited to the incarnation accounts for nearly all the biblical references that suggest subordination. Although it may seem obvious that verses regarding the Son's incarnation should not be assumed to describe his eternal relationship with the Father, as Augustine points out, such interpretations have caused considerable confusion. "Things are so said in the sacred books as to signify, or even most expressly declare, the Father to be greater than the Son; men have erred through a want of careful examination or consideration of the whole tenor of the Scriptures, and have endeavored to transfer those things which are said of Jesus Christ according to the flesh, to that substance of His which was eternal before the incarnation, and is eternal."[25] Obviously, debates about correct biblical interpretation are nothing new. But Augustine was clear that statements in the Bible ascribing the Son's subordination during his incarnation should not be confused with his eternal status. Although the doctrine of the Trinity is not spelled out as such in the Bible, we can see its basis as well as sense its mystery in the biblical passages mentioned above.

In this chapter we have looked at the purpose and methods of Paul's ministry and we have considered passages dealing with women in ministry, headship, and the Trinity. Although both complementarians and egalitarians take the Bible seriously, I believe the egalitarian perspective shows a better understanding of Paul's purpose and better represents the God of the Bible.

So far we have explored the current theological debate between egalitarians and complementarians, the church's historical view regarding subordination, and what the Bible says about male/female relationships and the relationship between the Father and the Son within the Trinity. In the remainder of this book, we will clarify some of the concepts we have been discussing and see how they might play out in our day to day lives. Chapter 8 will focus on submission.

25. Augustine, *On the Trinity*, 1:14.

8

Submission: Who Does It?

I'VE HEARD both men and women refer to submission as the "S" word. Christian women shy from the word because it has often been used to "keep them in their place." Christian men hesitate to use the word because they anticipate a negative reaction from women. And that's the problem. Frequently both Christian men and women assume submission is a female issue. In reality, both men and women are called to humility and submission.

I am defining submission as voluntary compliance, the act of yielding or surrendering to the power, authority, or wishes of another. The Bible talks about submission across the spectrum. It is true there are scriptures that specifically instruct wives to submit to their husbands (Eph 5:22; Col 3:18) and those who are younger to submit to their elders (1 Pet 5:5). But beyond that, all Christians are called to serve and submit to one another (Eph 5:21; Gal 5:13), to submit to those in authority (1 Pet 2:13), and, ultimately, of course, to submit to God (Jas 4:7). All Christians are called to submission.

SUBMISSION IS COSTLY

The Bible instructs us to humble ourselves (Matt 18:4, 23:12; Jas 4:10); to clothe ourselves with humility (Col 3:12); and to walk humbly with God (Mic 6:8). Apparently God understands that humility doesn't come naturally to us because alongside the call to humility is the promise that those who humble themselves will be given special grace (Prov 3:34; James 4:4–6) and that in the end the humble will be exalted. Although submission and humility are Christian trademarks to which we should all aspire, they are not traits to which we naturally gravitate. And I don't believe—as some claim—that submission comes more naturally to women then to men. On the contrary, it is a significant challenge for any of us to live lives marked by submission and humility.

Jesus is our ultimate example and, as we know, even for the Son of God—perhaps *especially* for the Son of God—submission was costly. Philippians 2:3–8 is an important passage to look at in this regard. First, it is significant because it witnesses to Jesus' recognition of his equality with God the Father. Second, it points out that although Jesus was God and equal with God, he voluntarily set aside his equality in order to carry out his redemptive earthly ministry. Third, Jesus' attitude of submission and humility is set before us as a model we should imitate. It is this third aspect of the passage that I want to look at in this chapter.

Jesus models the attitude we are to have toward one another. As human beings, we share the equality of our humanity. We are all created in the image of God and have inherent value and worth. But according to Philippians 2, that equality is not something to which we should cling. Nor is it something we should deny. Rather, acknowledging our equality with one another, we are to imitate Christ and live out humility, obedience, and submissiveness in our day-to-day interactions with each other. I understand that to mean that women should not grasp for equality and men should not grasp for superiority. Instead, both men and women should humble themselves—even sacrifice themselves—in obedience to God.

SUBMISSION IS FOR BOTH MEN AND WOMEN

I have heard people argue that while Paul admonishes men to love their wives and wives to submit to their husbands, he nowhere commands wives to love their husbands or husbands to submit to their wives. Seriously? In the instructions Paul gives both men and women in Philippians 2, he uses the same example of Jesus' sacrificial life that he uses in Ephesians 5:25 when writing only to husbands. In Philippians Paul says that all Christians are to humble themselves and to live sacrificially. In John 15:12, Jesus commands all Christians to love one another. It doesn't say that women are supposed to love everyone except their husbands. Nor does the Bible suggest that out of reverence for Christ men are to submit to everyone except their wives. It is ludicrous to separate Paul's instructions to wives and husbands in a way that implies men are never called to submission and women are not called to love.

So although it's true that a few biblical passages are addressed specifically to men and others specifically to women, according to Philippians 2 and John 15, both men and women are called to have Christlike attitudes and to love, respect, sacrifice, and submit to one another. The overall message of the Bible is addressed to both men and women and specific instructions to one or the other do not override the basic message of the gospel.

I make this point because it is easy to read the Bible selectively. I started out believing the whole Bible was meant for me. However, during the 1970s, as I tried to be a good, submissive, total, and fascinating woman, scripture narrowed down into an oppressive impossible-to-live-out extrapolation of select passages. Unfortunately, I am not the only woman who has felt stuck in a biblical quagmire.

Sarah Sumner tells an interesting experience she had while speaking at a Christian women's conference. Her text was Matthew 18:15–16, the passage that tells how to confront those who have sinned against us. Sumner posed the following question: "Does Matthew 18 apply to wives?" Sumner says the women in the room looked around at each other in stunned silence. What was she talking about? One of the women said, "I have never had a thought about Matthew 18. I mean, I've thought about it before, but not within the context of marriage. I've always been taught that wives are supposed to win their husbands 'without a word' [1 Pet 3:1]. I thought I had to be silent."[1] Sumner concludes that although the Bible clearly lays out a process by which Christians can confront one another, the women didn't think it applied to them. The women in the room honestly believed that as wives, they had no recourse other than prayer by which to hold their husbands accountable. They had it in their minds that "chaste and respectful behavior" (1 Pet 3:2) precluded them from speaking the truth (Eph 4:15).[2]

The women to whom Sumner was speaking took passages such as Paul's specific instructions to wives regarding submission and silence and, instead of recognizing them as part of Paul's overall message regarding submission to one another, lifted them out and laid them over the entire Bible, cutting themselves off from the biblical truth and recourse meant for all Christians.

Just as some Christian women don't recognize their options, some Christian men don't recognize their obligations. Sumner points out that Christian men sometimes see wifely submission as an entitlement issue—they are entitled to their wives' submission. She tells the story about a man who had instructed his wife to always bathe after he had taken his shower so that he would never be without hot water. When Sumner asked him if he thought this was an example of what it meant for his wife to submit, he reflexively responded that he thought it was. Sumner relates that he understood he was called to sacrifice for his wife, but he apparently thought of sacrifice as something on a greater scale. "Thus he told himself—and us—that he would die for her. He did not tell himself that he would sacrifice the luxury of taking a hot shower so that she could enjoy a hot bath." Sumner goes on: "Many Christian men honestly believe that headship is the equivalent of entitlement. They feel entitled as the head because that is what they have been taught."[3]

---

1. Sumner, *Men and Women,* 195–96.
2. Ibid., 197–98.
3. Ibid., 198–99.

I have participated in enough women's Bible studies over the years to know that that is what many women have been taught as well. Women sit around for hours trying to figure out how to submit to husbands who are behaving in selfish and self-centered ways. Although they feel frustrated and helpless, they rarely acknowledge that the way their husbands are treating them is sinful. Ignoring their husbands' sin, they carry both the hope that they can, and the burden that they should, be able to work things out for themselves. If they can just keep silent or find the right words or cultivate the right tone of voice maybe things will get better. Under the circumstances, their time would be better spent focusing on forgiveness than on submission.

Some of the confusion surrounding the issue of submission stems from Ephesians 5:22–33. Christian women who desperately want their marriages to "work" focus almost entirely on verse twenty-two in which Paul exhorts wives to submit to their husbands. In an attempt to better understand the passage, I outlined it and read through it slowly again and again. As I read and reread my outline, trying to understand the whole meaning, not just the first verse about wives submitting to their husbands, I was amazed that this passage could ever seem oppressive to women. But as I said, I have participated in enough women's Bible studies to know that it often *is* oppressive. I believe the reason is exactly what Sumner so vividly illustrates with her hot water story. Both men and women recognize there are hundreds of nitty-gritty opportunities for wives to submit to their husbands each day. On the other hand, opportunities for husbands to sacrifice for their wives are seen as remote, once-in-a-lifetime, life or death situations that few encounter. If the idea of sacrifice were thrown up to men as often as submission has been thrown up to women, we might have a new "S" word.

SUBMISSION IN A FALLEN WORLD

In her book, *Gender and Grace,* Mary Stewart Van Leeuwen speaks to the way the fall into sin has impacted the human condition. "I have argued that the Fall seems to have had somewhat different effects on men and women in general, men becoming more prone to turn dominion into domination and women more prone to turn sociability into social enmeshment of an unhealthy sort."[4] I believe Van Leeuwen is correct.

Throughout history elaborate social structures, inventions, and norms have been established to help us cope with the conditions outlined at the time of the Fall in Genesis. These are coping mechanisms, not God-given ordinances. Some of them have proven helpful; some have shown themselves to be wrong-headed. I would not personally turn down a pain killer during childbirth, but that's a personal choice. The fact that I might need a painkiller in the first place is an acknowledgement of fallen reality.

A patriarchal social system is one of the ways men and women have used to cope with gender conflicts resulting from the Fall. Today we live in an updated milder version of a system that dates back to the Old Testament patriarchs. The establishment of slavery is another way those in control have coped with the sweat and painful toil involved in making a living in a fallen world. Van Leeuwen compares the gender issue with the issue of slavery and says that both issues must be considered within the broad scope of the Bible as well as within the movement of history.

For many years Christians justified slavery on scriptural grounds, but today most Christians see slavery as repulsive rather than part of a God-given social order. The top down social system that has so dominated society throughout the centuries is similarly a man-made coping structure. It is not the ideal way for men and women to live and work together in the kingdom of God and in the church today.

4. Van Leeuwen, *Gender,* 248.

Van Leeuwen makes an interesting distinction between what she calls the "pilgrim principle" and the "missionary principal." The pilgrim principal reminds us that God's people will always be somewhat at odds with the culture around them. God's people are in the world but not of the world (1 Pet 2:11: John 17:13–16; 1 Pet 1:17). At the same time, the missionary principle means that "for the sake of advancing God's kingdom in a given time and place, temporary compromises can and often must be made with the societal status quo."[5] In a previous chapter we saw how determined Paul was to not let anything stand in the way of the spread of the gospel (Acts 16:3; 1 Cor 6:6, 8:1–13, 10:31–33). Paul was applying the missionary principle. At the same time, he was a visionary and knew that accommodating the culture in which he lived was not the end of the story. Van Leeuwen understands this as well. "Thus the early church, even while tolerating slavery for the sake of the missionary principle, pointed to a vision of Christian justice and community which would eventually leave slavery behind."[6] She argues that in a similar manner the Bible points beyond patriarchy to "a vision of mutuality between brothers and sisters in Christ in marriage, church and society."[7] Van Leeuwen warns that this may call for traditionalists to change the way they think and act. But at the same time, she warns that progressives must also make concessions and "adjust the achievement of justice for ourselves to the larger agenda of advancing God's kingdom in a given historical setting." She adds that "both women and men are sometimes called to set aside their 'just deserts,' however responsibly each may be reading these from the Bible. Like Christ himself, they must be willing to become servants for the sake of the kingdom."[8]

Similarly, Kevin Giles, commenting on Philippians 2, notes that at times both men and women may need to give up what is

5. Van Leeuwen, *Gender,* 236.
6. Ibid., 239.
7. Ibid., 239.
8. Ibid., 249.

rightfully theirs in order to live out a Christlike attitude. He says, "Preserving one's privileges, holding on to power, is not Christlike."[9] The role Jesus played on earth was a role he took upon himself and was willing to carry out. It was a concession to the condition of fallen humanity in order to carry out God's overall plan of redemption for the people he loved. Likewise, women, while understanding they are God's image-bearers and equal to men in both essence and function, may accommodate themselves to a lesser role in order to carry out and not hamper the redemptive purpose of the church. This does not mean they are in an permanent, subordinate position below men, but that in attempting to be Christlike in their attitude they subject themselves to the conditions of our fallen world.

I believe it was this frame of mind that colored the initial response of my friend, Barbara, when I asked her about women in ministry. Barbara Fletcher is Associate Pastor at our church and is on a regular preaching rotation schedule with the lead pastor and two or three others. I asked her what positions she believed it was OK for women to hold in the church. She quickly responded, "Any position except senior pastor." I was surprised at her response because I thought she believed that all ministries were open to women. But then she went on to explain that her response was because of our culture, not because she believes the Bible prohibits women from being senior pastors. She is sensitive to the divisiveness and confusion that placing a woman in a senior pastor position would most likely cause within our denomination and probably within many evangelical churches today. I believe her attitude is exactly what Paul is speaking to in Philippians 2:5–11. She recognizes her equality with men and others recognize that she is gifted in teaching and administration. She has not, however, "grasped" that equality in terms of church office. It is one thing to knock on a door, and then as it opens, walk through it. It is something else to kick the door down. I don't believe Barbara would have arrived at her current position as pastor of adult ministries if she

9. Giles, *Trinity*, 116–17.

had not knocked on some doors, but she certainly has not kicked any down. She recognizes the fallen condition of our world and is sensitive to the realities of our evangelical culture.

In a similar vein, Jesus' subordination during the incarnation is a concession to our humanity and to the reality of our fallen nature—to our need of a savior. There is a thread linking the suffering and submission of Christ in the face of our fallen human condition and the results of the fall as predicted in the Garden of Eden. God predicted that men would rule over women. One result was the establishment of the elaborate patriarchal system we read about in the Old Testament. Remnants of that system remain to this day. Sometimes this system served to protect the powerless, but no matter who holds power, there is the propensity to abuse it. It is this tendency of those who have power to use it against those who do not that makes power and submission such a dicey issue. How can we, as Christians, live lives marked by humility and submission? How can we be righteous in our exercise of power?

SUBMISSION AS A WAY OF LIFE

The most vivid word for me in Philippians 2 is the word *grasped*— "Christ Jesus . . . did not consider equality with God something to be grasped." That word brings to my mind all the times I have gritted my teeth and felt my stomach churn as I determined to get something I deserved, or thought I deserved, or knew I didn't deserve but wanted anyway. Perhaps the reason this passage strikes me so profoundly is because it is not an abstract concept about God becoming human, but something that has a direct bearing upon how I live my life. Paul uses it as an example for us. Jesus' incarnation, his coming into our world as a human like us, is crucial to our believing that we too can humble ourselves, be obedient to God, and serve each other. It is also crucial to our understanding that we live in a fallen world and that, instead of merely resigning ourselves to the distortions of the culture in which we live, we should make the changes we can.

In Galatians 3:26–28, Paul powerfully describes the new life in Christ that makes it possible to leave our old power structures and coping mechanisms behind. Our oneness in Christ trumps ethnic, racial, social, and gender differences. Some theologians insist that this passage relates only to salvation and does not have social implications. While it may be legitimate to say that Paul's primary point in this passage has to do with salvation, it is foolish to suggest this passage has no social implications whatsoever. At the very least, we can say that Christians should not be using differences such as these against one another. Unfortunately, even that minimal understanding of the passage has been violated again and again in the history of the church.

Marva J. Dawn speaks to this. "If all the created powers tend, in this fallen world, to overstep their bounds—and if the Church and its servants are called instead to weakness so that the power of God may tabernacle in us—then it is important for us to notice in what ways churches live as fallen powers or function out of biblical *sarx* (flesh) instead of the Spirit."[10] I don't believe Galatians 3:26–28 wipes out all differences between men and women, but I certainly believe it has social and ecclesiastical implications. Although it doesn't specify church offices or spell out what kinds of leadership positions women may hold, it suggests volumes about the attitude of respect, honor, and acceptance that we as Christians are to extend to one another.

As we noted earlier, slavery is one of the means used by those with power to cope with the sweat and toil resulting from the fall. In the book of Philemon, when Paul urges Philemon to receive his run-away slave, Onesimus, as a brother in Christ, he is suggesting how our oneness in Christ might impact a social institution such as slavery. Clearly Paul hoped their relationship as brothers in Christ would have an influence on their relationship as slave and slave holder. In his commentary on Philemon, Maxie D. Dunnam points out that Jesus made a direct connection between our relationship with him and the way we treat others. "Some of Jesus' harshest words of

10. Dawn, *Powers, Weakness*, 73.

condemnation were reserved for 'religious' men who vainly thought their worship of God, their 'church' life, could be separated from their life in the world."[11] We violate our calling to live out our salvation in our world if we compartmentalize our lives in such a way that we separate our salvation from our lifestyle.

Years ago I was powerfully struck by Philippians 2:6–7, by Paul's description of Christ, "Who, being in very nature God, did not consider equality with God something to be grasped, but made himself nothing, taking the very nature of a servant, being made in human likeness." I was struck by what it might mean for me to follow Christ's example, what it might mean for women with God-given equality to live in a fallen world in which that equality is frequently not recognized. Today Paul's call to Christlike submission continues to challenge me.

I want to close this chapter with a quote by Gretchen Gaebelein Hull. In a chapter titled, "Saved to Serve Together," written over twenty years ago, Hull talks about serving with a Christlike attitude. She succinctly captures what struck me so powerfully many years ago. Hull addresses women with both compassion and challenge.

> Can you drink the cup of submission? Yes, I realize full well what many of you are thinking: That's all we've ever done. But I would ask of you: Can you now drink the cup as Christ means you to drink it? Not because you must, but because you choose to? Would you be willing to put aside your legitimate rights, if the time to exercise them is not yet right in your particular circumstances? Would you be willing to put your career on hold, if that is in the best interests of your family or your cultural milieu? Will you work for change in a patient and loving manner, rather than sinking into anger or bitterness? Will you commit yourself to work in a Christ-like way, even if you are in un-Christ-like situations?[12]

I think those questions, more than any others, are the right questions for women to ask themselves in regard to submission.

They are the right questions for men to ask as well.

11. Dunnam, *Philemon,* 409. Italics in this quote are Dunnam's.
12. Hull, *Equal to Serve,* 241.

9

Authority: Who Has It?

In the previous chapter we explored submission and I pointed out that God calls both men and women to submission and humility. In a similar manner, in this chapter we will see that both men and women are gifted by God and entrusted with spiritual authority. In some ways this chapter mirrors my personal journey over the last twenty-five or thirty years. I have bumped along trying to make sense of my experience as an evangelical Christian woman who came of age at the dawn of the feminist movement, struggled through the Christian backlash, took timid steps out of total womanhood, and finally settled in as a wary egalitarian. My presuppositions have been challenged all along the way. Throughout this book we have been exploring the functional and essential equality of women. In this chapter we will look at how that equality impacts our understanding of spiritual authority.

WHAT DO WE MEAN BY AUTHORITY?

It has always been a curiosity to me that many Christians take seriously Paul's admonition in 1 Timothy 2:11–12 against women teaching or assuming authority over men, while essentially ignoring the reason he gives. Paul says that women should not teach or have authority over men for "it was the woman who was deceived and became a sinner" (I Tim 2:14). If it is true that women are more easily deceived than men, then it is unconscionable to allow easily deceived women to teach other easily deceived women. It is even more shameful to allow easily deceived women to teach impressionable young children. It troubles me that we can explain away or ignore the deception part of this verse, but cling tenaciously to the restriction about women teaching men.

A number of years ago I was visiting with a pastor friend who, based on 1 Timothy 2:12–14, believed women should never teach the Bible to men. I asked him why he thought easily deceived women could teach children and other women, but could not teach men. After all, men should be able to hold their own. He brushed my words aside. "Well, no, it's not a matter of deception; it's a matter of authority." The look on his face and the tone of his voice indicated the matter was settled. But it was clear to me then, and is still clear to me today, that any adult Sunday school teacher who teaches children—in the children's minds at least—has spiritual authority.

The problem with the *spiritual authority* argument is that it is hard to know what it means. The issue of authority—who has it, how we get it, and what it entails—is not always clear. Is it based on age . . . formal office . . . gender? Common sense tells us that authority—spiritual or otherwise—can be rooted in a variety of things. Some people have authority because of their office or official position. Some have it because of their personal charisma. Some have it because people recognize their wisdom or integrity. In the Bible we often see God anointing people with spiritual authority because of their obedience to Him. But it seems to me that much of the current debate on spiritual authority is related to official positions of authority rather than to authority based on obedience, wisdom, or integrity.

Most complementarians seem content to allow women to minister as long as they don't encroach on specific official positions such as elder, senior pastor, or teacher. The role of senior pastor is not a position or office named in scripture, so that particular limitation is not biblically based. Although limitations on eldership and teaching can be argued from scripture, one suspects that tradition and maintenance of the status quo also play a part. For some it is personal preference—one woman admitted to me that she didn't like listening to women preach because she didn't like the sound of women's voices. Others acknowledge it is an issue of institutional power and structure. Whatever the reasons given, it is often difficult to identify the real issue.

I believe it is difficult for both men and women in evangelical communities to separate tradition, the status quo, and what is comfortable, from a critical analysis of biblical assumptions. In many cases—perhaps most—I believe limitations are placed on the ministry of women out of a sincere desire to remain true to what the Bible teaches. Unfortunately, it is all too easy to fall into the patterns of the culture in which we live and confuse social convention with biblical truth. At times it is even difficult to truly "get" the fact that God is neither male nor female. Unexamined assumptions die hard.

AUTHORITY AND BIBLICAL INTERPRETATION

Until the 1970s, when I first read *All We're Meant to Be*, by Letha Scanzoni and Nancy Hardesty, I had assumed God's words to the woman in Genesis 3:16—"Your desire will be for your husband, and he will rule over you"—were part of God's original plan, his ideal for husband/wife relationships. It had never occurred to me that those words were a result of the Fall, part of the curse following the disobedience of Adam and Eve.[1] But once it was pointed out, it seemed obvious and I was surprised that I had never noticed it before. Just recently I mentioned this to an acquaintance and she looked as surprised as I had felt three decades ago. "I guess I've never thought of it that way," she said. "But I'm not sure it's God's curse . . . maybe a consequence."

"Well, curse or consequence," I said, "it is not God's ideal."

I could tell she wasn't convinced. A short time later I had a similar experience with a young husband and father, a graduate

1. Scanzoni and Hardesty, *Meant to Be*, 35.

of a Christian college who was active in church ministry. We were talking about the meaning of the word helpmeet. He was surprised when I told him that the Hebrew word translated helpmeet in Genesis 2:18 is often used in the Old Testament in the context of God as our helper and that it carries no inherent connotations of inferiority or servitude. He had the same blank look on his face. "Really?" he said, "I've never heard that before."

At this point in my life I take those bits of information about the creation story in Genesis for granted and assume that most thinking Christians—while not necessarily agreeing—have at least grappled with the possibility that the creation narrative does not establish male priority. Apparently that is not true.

As Protestants, we like to think we base our beliefs on the Bible rather than on tradition. However, in reality, we are often bound up in unexamined presuppositions and it is difficult to break away from them. Our assumptions about who should lead, who has spiritual authority, and what words should be in our Bibles are often based as much upon what we are used to as on sound biblical translation and exegesis. A careful study of the Bible can lead us to question some of our favorite presuppositions, one of them being who has spiritual authority and who doesn't. My personal study of the Bible has led me to the conclusion that, for the most part, spiritual authority is not based on social status, gender, or church office. Instead, I believe that God lavishes spiritual authority on those who trust and obey him—both men and women.

AUTHORITY AND PERSONAL EXPERIENCE

I went through a period of trying to be a totally submissive woman. At the time I was a stay-at-home mom and had my hands full with three pre-schoolers. In some ways I liked the idea of being "under my husband's umbrella." I didn't have to take responsibility for anything. I didn't have to think. I didn't have to feel. All I had to do was smile and nod. However, I was temperamentally unable to keep that up for very long. In addition, in spite of all the "umbrella" talk I was convinced that God would hold me, not my husband, responsible for what I did with my life.

In 1 Corinthians 15:58, Paul says, "Therefore, my dear brothers, stand firm. Let nothing move you. Always give yourselves fully to the work of the Lord, because you know that your labor in the Lord is not in vain." When I read that verse—even in a version that was not gender inclusive—I understood that those words were intended for me just as much as they were intended for any man. But when I was in my trying-hard-to-be-submissive phase, I did not feel that same responsibility toward God. I felt responsible only to my husband. The result was a shrinking of self and a huge barrier between me and God. It wasn't that my husband was not a spiritual man or worthy of my respect and honor. He was and is. It was that placing him between me and God distanced me from God and from his call on my life. It was a form of idolatry that separated me from God and placed unrealistic expectations on my husband. How could I make sense of both my womanhood and God's call upon my life?

Living on the Boundaries is a book that accurately describes the circumstances in which egalitarians and evangelical feminists find themselves today. The authors, Nicola Hoggard Creegan and Christine D. Pohl surveyed eighty-nine women in the academic fields of theology, missions, biblical studies, church history, and ethics. They all identify themselves, or once identified themselves, as evangelicals. Creegan and Pohl point out that, "Feminist theology written from the perspective of evangelical women has been largely absent."[2] They wrote their book to fill that gap. It is interesting to me because it explores the world in which I live. The authors note that evangelicals and feminists are most often perceived as opposing groups. The authors' interviews with women who considered themselves both evangelicals and feminists were enlightening. Many of the women found themselves in places that

2. Creegan and Pohl, *Living on the Boundaries*, 28.

were uncomfortable and confusing. They were taking both their life experiences and God's word seriously and were trying to find the common truth. In my desire to fit into a conservative, evangelical culture, I have often fallen into the trap of dismissing my own experience and the experiences of other women as insignificant or wrong-headed.

I have long felt that if we read the Bible and there is no way to relate what we read to what we have personally experienced—and there is no understanding that there should be a relationship there—then our lives are irrelevant. The fact that it can be difficult to live in both worlds—the world of evangelicalism as well as the world of egalitarianism—makes the issue real, something to be examined and reckoned with. I think God expects each of us to integrate what we know of him through the Bible and the Holy Spirit with what we know because of our life experiences.

In *Exploring Our Christian Faith,* W.T. Purkiser quotes John Owen, who makes an interesting observation in this regard. He points out how God's revelation of himself and the response he desires from mankind have been different at different times. Before Christ the "testing truth" was God's oneness and sovereignty. After Jesus came, receiving him as the incarnate Son was a sign of orthodoxy. Today it is the recognition of the person and power of the Holy Spirit. Owen said that rejecting the person and work of the Holy Spirit now, "is of the same nature with the idolatry of old, and with the Jews' rejection of the Person of the Son."[3] To me, the relevance of the above quote is the suggestion that at different times in history God has expected his followers to respond in different ways—ways that are dependent upon the way God has revealed himself in the day in which they lived. Underlying this suggestion is the assumption that God is at work in us in the time and place in which we live and that the God-events in our lives are important.

Our task is not to use culture as an excuse to water down or ignore biblical texts which make us uncomfortable. Rather our

3. Purkiser, "The Holy Spirit," 165–67.

task is to examine the culture in which they were written, as well as the culture in which we live, to better understand how to apply the truth today. We should not expect Paul to be "politically correct" by today's standards. But today we *are* responsible, not to be politically correct, but to be sensitive to injustices and scriptural distortions that have been tolerated in the past. As we have seen in previous chapters, what the Church has believed about women and about the Trinity has been colored by time and culture. What is the Holy Spirit teaching the church today about slavery, women, and the Trinity? We are responsible to understand what God is trying to teach us in our day.

The apostles experienced the life, death, and resurrection of Jesus. Today we experience the work of the Holy Spirit. In addition to the Holy Spirit alive in us, we have experienced events in our lifetimes through which previous generations have not lived. In my lifetime I have been exposed to the sexual revolution, the civil rights movement, and the feminist movement. While some of these events have had a negative impact on the morality of our culture, others have brought attention to injustices tolerated in the past. There are lies and distortions rampant in today's culture. But there are truths as well. If we are fortunate enough to discern biblical priorities on the move in our culture—as is certainly the case in regard to the civil rights movement—we are responsible to pay attention to that and get on board.

The Bible is our highest authority. However, we must also take our personal life experiences seriously. When we obey God in the midst of the time and culture in which we live and within the context of our work, family, church, and interpersonal circumstances, he imbues us with the spiritual authority to impact others.

AUTHORITY AND SPIRITUAL GIFTS

Few of us would maintain that God has limited certain gifts of the Spirit to one gender or the other. Some men have the gift of mercy; some women have the gift of administration. Some women are gifted in evangelism and some men are gifted in teaching. Paul taught that the gifts of the Spirit were distributed for the common good (1 Cor 12:7) as the Spirit chose (1 Cor 12:11) without discrimination. "For in the one Spirit we were all baptized into one body—Jews or Greeks, slaves or free—and we were made to drink of one Spirit" (1 Cor 12:13). Paul never suggests that the Spirit limits who can get which gifts. There is no gender bias.

Although God distributes spiritual gifts to men and women alike, there are those who believe they know where, when, and by whom certain gifts should be exercised. This is particularly true of complementarians in regard to the gift of teaching. When House discusses what kind of speaking women may and may not do in the church, he takes the position that although it is OK for women to prophesy and pray in church, it is not OK for them to teach men. He makes a careful distinction between prophecy and preaching. He recognizes that Paul assumed women would prophesy, but denies that this means women can also preach or teach God's word. He quotes Oscar Cullman who makes the distinction that prophecy is "based on direct revelation" whereas preaching is "founded on an intelligible exposition of the Word of God."[4] He goes on to say, "Preaching in the church is honored over prophecy in Paul's writings because of its strategic place in God's economy, and Paul reserves it for men."[5]

In addition to being questionable whether Paul elevates preaching over prophecy (1 Cor 1:1), this kind of hair splitting is in direct opposition to the point Paul is trying to make about respect and interdependency within the body of Christ (Rom 12:3–5). We see a similar stretch in the way D.A. Carson approaches I Corinthians 14:33–36. He briefly explains eight ways to interpret this passage, ranging all the way from those who believe the demand for the silence of women is absolute to those who ascribe

4. House, *Role of Women in Ministry*, 114.

5. Ibid., 115.

the quote to the Corinthians with whom Paul is arguing. Carson determines that Paul's instructions regarding the silence of women have to do with the evaluation of prophecy. Although women are allowed to prophecy themselves, they are not allowed to evaluate the prophecies of others.[6] He says that "a strong case can be made for the view that Paul refused to permit any woman to enjoy a church-recognized teaching authority over men (1 Tim 2:11ff.), and the careful weighing of prophecies falls under that magisterial function."[7] He could be right about that, I suppose, but to me the reasoning seems strained.

I think we need to recognize that in this passage dealing with orderly worship, most of us are not nearly as concerned about every other jot and tittle in these verses as we are about the possible restrictions placed on the rights of women to speak. When evangelical churches meet on Sunday morning it is typically not the case that "everyone has a hymn, or a word of instruction, a revelation, a tongue or an interpretation." Instead, the choir sings the songs they practiced Wednesday night, the congregation joins in the praise choruses selected by the music director, and the senior pastor is the only one who brings a word of instruction. If someone should stand up and claim to have a revelation, he or she might be quietly ushered out, and, except in Pentecostal churches, if anyone should speak in tongues, he or she would more likely be met by an embarrassing silence than an interpretation. Most evangelical churches have developed their own patterns of worship with little concern about Paul's description in this passage. It is obvious to most evangelicals that Paul's main concern in this passage is orderly worship and that it is not necessary to slavishly follow every detail Paul describes. Paul is addressing order and propriety issues in Corinth and women were apparently part of the problem. Paul decides they need to be quiet. What is the justification for taking

6. Carson, "Silent in the Churches," 143–53.

7. Ibid., 152.

this one aspect of the passage and applying it to our churches today while basically ignoring other worship details described here?

There is no indication that the spiritual gifts listed in 1Corinthians 12 and Romans 12—including the gifts of teaching, leadership, and prophecy—are in any way assigned according to gender. It is apparent that God has gifted both men and women to teach and to lead. Although having certain gifts does not mean they should be used in every context, placing restrictions on gifted women—just because they are women—is to waste a God-given resource. If women are equal to men in function as well as essence—and I believe they are—then it does not seem that gender is a legitimate basis for limiting the way women exercise their gifts of teaching or administration.

AUTHORITY AND LEADERSHIP

Women held a number of leadership positions in the early church. However, in light of the pagan culture in Ephesus, it is no surprise to me that when Paul lists the qualifications for overseers and deacons in 1 Timothy 3:2, he includes the stipulation that anyone seeking to be an overseer must be the "husband of one wife." This does not necessarily mean Paul is taking a position against female leadership in the Ephesian church. The wording he used may just be the most natural way of saying that overseers should be people of integrity and not given to loose living. It is easy to see how this might be. In the United States, as of this writing in 2010, we have yet to elect a woman as President. During the sex scandals of Bill Clinton's administration, it would not have been a surprise to hear frustrated conservatives proclaim that a President of the United States should at least be a man of character and faithful to his wife. Would this mean that women are forbidden from the Presidency? Of course not. It would simply be the most natural way of saying that we want our Presidents to be persons of integrity. To check this out, I surveyed 93 college freshmen, asking them to respond to the following hypothetical scenario: *During the Clinton administration sex scandal a well-known conservative Republican called a news conference. He made this statement: "The President of the United States should be a man of integrity and faithful to his wife." A liberal Democratic Senator called a news conference the next day and lambasted the Republican for suggesting that a woman should never be President. Headlines read: "Right-wing senator suggests Presidency limited to males."*

I asked the students what they believed the Republican senator was trying to say. Was he saying that (a) The President of the United States should be a person of integrity, or was he saying that (b) A woman should never be President of the United States? Ninety-two of the ninety-three students surveyed indicated that the senator was speaking to the integrity of the President, not to whether or not a woman should be President.

I think something similar is going on in 1 Timothy. I believe Paul's intent in this passage is to lay out the character qualifications of leaders, not to mandate whether they are male or female.

In Paul's other writings, particularly those regarding spiritual gifts and those referring to the church as the body of Christ, he places a strong emphasis on Christians working together. Each part of the body makes a contribution to the healthy functioning of the whole. Phelan points out that the church needs female leaders as well as male leaders to function at its best. While acknowledging the danger of identifying certain qualities as uniquely female and others as masculine, he says that, "it is interesting that the method of leadership recommended by the New Testament is more often identified in our culture with the way *women* lead—nurturing, persuading, cooperating, and coming alongside."[8] He goes on to say that these leadership qualities are "critically needed these days in the church."[9]

---

8. Phelan, *God's People,* 71.

9. Ibid.

God has gifted both men and women with special abilities to lead, teach, prophesy, serve, encourage, give, and extend mercy. Paul is clear that all these gifts need to be at work in the church. I think we misunderstand what Paul is trying to say when we take his remarks regarding women and use them to limit the way women are allowed to exercise their gifts.

AUTHORITY AND LANGUAGE

I was in the second or third grade—probably the second, because I can remember where I was seated, on the left side of the four-grade classroom where first and second graders sat—when my teacher explained about personal pronouns. The male pronoun *he* was used in reference to both boys and girls. I rarely asked questions in front of the whole class, but I raised my hand.

"Why?" I asked.

The teacher paused for a brief moment, then, using that tone of voice that discourages further inquiry, replied with something along the lines of, "That's just the way it is." I remember a heaviness settling over me.

This was big.

It was in the language.

I am grateful for that memory. It comes to my mind whenever I hear people argue that inclusive language is not important. If not for that memory, I might agree. But instead I know that it *is* important. It was important to me as a grade-schooler. In morose moments I wonder how many times my childhood recognition that it was *in the language* caused me to underestimate the value of what I was thinking or made me brush aside the relevance of my ideas. All I know is something clicked inside my brain in that moment back in the second or third grade—something I wasn't able to verbalize but have never been able to forget.

In *Distorting Scripture?*, Mark L. Strauss chronicles the controversy surrounding gender inclusive translations of the Bible. He notes that some Christians believe that using inclusive language in biblical translations is "an inappropriate capitulation to the feminist agenda."[10] He goes on to say, "The real issue is not whether gender-inclusive language is related to the women's movement (it certainly is) but whether such language accurately conveys the intention of the original author."[11] That some Christians are more concerned with opposing the "feminist agenda" than they are with rendering an accurate and inclusive translation of scripture is a sad commentary on the way lines have been drawn within Christianity in regard to women. Strauss, himself a complementarian, defends gender inclusive language when "that language demonstrably represents the biblical author's intended meaning. This perspective is not based on a social or political feminist agenda (I oppose such an agenda) but on the nature of language and translation."[12]

I agree with Strauss. Biblical translations should include inclusive language when it helps clarify the biblical author's original meaning. Perhaps there was a time when most people understood and accepted that male pronouns included both male and female. But for the most part, that time has passed. When done unintentionally, out of habit or laziness, using the male pronoun to encompass references to both men and women may just indicate thoughtlessness. But language is a powerful tool. The intentional rejection of inclusive language serves to undermine the authority and relevance of women. Today most people consider it insensitive to spurn gender inclusive language.

AUTHORITY AND PRIESTHOOD

While reading through the Old Testament a few years ago, I was astonished to see parallels between the Kohathites and the traditional role of women. The Kohathites were sons of Levi, charged

10. Strauss, *Distorting Scripture?* 16.
11. Ibid.
12. Ibid., 25.

with caring for the sanctuary of the Tent of Meeting. "They were responsible for the care of the ark, the table, the lampstand, the altars, the articles of the sanctuary used in ministering, the curtain, and everything related to their use" (Num 3:28–30). Although the Kohathites were charged with caring for the items in the sanctuary, there were limits to their responsibilities. Moses and Aaron and Aaron's sons were also responsible for the sanctuary. But they held a higher responsibility. "They were responsible for the care of the sanctuary on behalf of the Israelites. Anyone else who approached the sanctuary was to be put to death" (Num 3:38). Not only are the Kohathites not to touch the holy things, they are not even to look at them (Num 4:20).

When it came time to move the Tent of Meeting, Aaron and his sons were to go into the sanctuary and cover all the most holy things with blue cloths. This was to protect the Kohathites. "After Aaron and his sons have finished covering the holy furnishings and all the holy articles, and when the camp is ready to move, the Kohathites are to come to do the carrying. But they must not touch the holy things or they will die. The Kohathites are to carry those things that are in the Tent of Meeting" (Num 4:5). So, while the Kohathites had an important ministry in regard to the Tent of Meeting, their ministry was restricted. They were not allowed to handle the holy things. Duties and responsibilities were assigned in an organized and orderly manner. Things should have run smoothly.

Unfortunately, Kohath, some other Levites, as well as some Reubenites, began to wonder why the very special, holy leadership responsibilities were reserved for Moses and Aaron. "They came as a group to oppose Moses and Aaron and said to them, 'You have gone too far! The whole community is holy, every one of them, and the LORD is with them. Why then do you set yourselves above the LORD's Assembly?'"

Moses responds by reminding them of the ministry God had given them. "Now listen, you Levites! Isn't it enough for you that God of Israel has separated you from the rest of the Israelite community and brought you near himself to do the work at the LORD's tabernacle and to stand before the community and minister to them? He has brought you and all your fellow Levites near himself, but now you are trying to get the priesthood too" (Num 16:8–10). Sound familiar?

Sometimes it seems that women are acting like the Kohathites. And complementarians join in the Kohathite drama when they say, "Look at all the ministries that are open to you! There are plenty of things for you to do in the church. Why do you think you also should be senior pastors? 'Are you trying to get the priesthood too?'"

Why indeed? Is it fair to compare women to the Kohathites? Are women who seek full ministry opportunities falling into the same trap as them?—reaching beyond their God-ordained responsibilities? It is perhaps this fear, more than any other that concerns those strongly defending the idea that God has ordained men for leadership roles that are not open to women.[13]

But what of this idea? What of the priesthood? What has happened to the whole priesthood concept? The role of priests was not only to care for the sanctuary articles. It was also up to them to offer sacrifices for the sins of the people. "Every high priest is selected from among men and is appointed to represent them in matters related to God, to offer gifts and sacrifices for sins. . . . No one takes this honor upon himself; he must be called by God, just as Aaron was" (Heb 5:1–4).

As Christians we believe that Jesus offered the perfect sacrifice once and for all, for all of us. The offerings once offered by the high priests are no longer necessary. What does this mean for us? What does it mean for women?—for Kohathites? "Therefore,

13. Borland suggests this. "Jesus' recognition of role distinctions for men and women is demonstrated by His choosing only men to serve as His apostles with the primary tasks of preaching, teaching, and governing. Women, however, served in other important capacities, such as praying, providing financial assistance, ministering to physical needs, voicing their theological understanding, and witness to the resurrection." Borland, "Women in the Life of Jesus," 113.

brothers and sisters, since we have confidence to enter the Most Holy Place by the blood of Jesus, by a new and living way opened for us through the curtain, that is, his body, and since we have a great priest over the house of God, let us draw near to God with a sincere heart in full assurance of faith, having our hearts sprinkled to cleanse us from a guilty conscience and having our bodies washed with pure water" (Heb 10:19–22, TNIV).

It seems that we are all free to enter into the Holy of Holies, to minister to God as priests—that all of us, men, women, Levites, Kohathites—are invited to draw near to God in a way unheard of back in the desert when the earth opened up and swallowed the Kohathites for presuming such a thing for themselves. This is confirmed by the Apostle Peter. "As you come to him, the living Stone—rejected by men but chosen by God and precious to him—you also, like living stones, are being built into a spiritual house to be a holy priesthood, offering spiritual sacrifices acceptable to God through Jesus Christ . . . . you are a chosen people, a royal priesthood, a holy nation, a people belonging to God, that you may declare the praises of him who called you out of darkness into his wonderful light" (I Pet 2:4,5, 9).

If we are to take Christ's work on the cross seriously, we must consider its impact in practical ways. Paul insists that we are all clothed in Christ—Jew, Greek, slave, free, male, and female.[14] We are all invited into the Holy of Holies; we are all "offering spiritual sacrifices acceptable to God through Jesus Christ."[15]

It is an affront to the work of Christ to reestablish the barriers he has broken down. God has gifted both men and women. God has imbued both men and women with spiritual authority. God has called both men and women into ministry. Christ died on the cross for all of humanity. Women are equal to men in both essence and function and limiting the ways in which women are encouraged and allowed to serve denies the efficacy of that work.

14. Galatians 3:28.
15. 1 Peter 2:5

10

Conclusion: What Is the Answer?

THE PURPOSE of this book has been to determine if permanent subordination in function on the one hand, and equality of essence on the other—whether applied to the Trinity or to the relationship between men and women—is a valid premise. While it is difficult to definitively either prove or disprove eternal subordination within the Trinity, we have seen that the argument is weighted heavily in favor of equality in both essence and function. At the same time, although the church has historically limited the ministry of women, and for many years women were considered inferior to men, a survey of biblical themes such as justice and mercy, an examination of Paul's writings, and a close look at Paul's use of the head and body metaphor support the permanent functional equality of women.

THE TRINITY

My study of subordination within the Trinity his convinced me there is more biblical and historical evidence to support the view that the Father and the Son are equal in both essence and function than there is to support the view that there is an eternal functional hierarchy within the Godhead. Have there been theologians in the past who have made a case for the eternal subordination of the Son? Certainly there have been. Some have made a case for ontological subordination and some have made a case for functional subordination. Everyone, of course, recognizes the subordination of the Son during the incarnation. However, it is my conclusion that if you say the Father and the Son have one will and are equal in their essence, their works, and their power, it is slicing things too thinly to then argue that the Son is eternally subordinate in function and authority. After studying many early theologians, I reject, and I believe the majority of theologians throughout church history would reject, the current theological argument that the Father and the Son are equal in essence, but that the Son is eternally subordinate in function and authority.

The biblical perspective on the incarnation and the Son's standing within the Godhead is nicely summed up by Paul in Phil 2:5–11. Jesus—very God—humbled himself, came to earth in human form, sacrificed himself for us, then returned to his former glory in heaven. Although there are a number of passages describing Jesus' obedience and submission to the Father, these must be understood in light of Jesus' incarnation, not in regard to his eternal standing within the Godhead. I believe the Bible teaches that God consists of the Father, Son, and Holy Spirit, one God in three persons, and that the persons of the Godhead are equal in both essence and function.

WOMEN

My study of the way women are viewed in the Bible and in church history has been both enlightening and challenging. I discovered that during the time of the New Testament and throughout church history there have been strong, influential women who have ministered in numerous ways. At the same time, theologians such as Ambrose, Calvin, and Barnes, considered women inferior and of lower rank than men. Others, such as Luther, Henry, and Hodge, believed that women should not be in positions of leadership and that they should be limited to—and satisfied with—their state of subjection. Although over the years women have exerted significant influence and have ministered effectively in evangelistic, social, and missionary work, historically they have been banned from the priesthood and often barred from church leadership. Some see this marginalization of women in a positive light, an upholding of God's biblical mandate that men are to lead and women are to follow. However, I see this marginalization of women as a result of sin and of reading scripture through a distorted lens.

In the Garden of Eden at the time of the Fall, God told Eve that her desire would be for her husband and that he would rule over her (Gen 3:16). This was a prediction of the reality in which we still live today. Many women spend their lives grasping for relationships that elude them and numerous men spend their lives seeking to control matters that go beyond their reach. The conflicting needs of women for relationship and men for control have distorted male/female relationships from the Garden of Eden to the present day. In some respects the patriarchal society described in the Old Testament, which included polygamy, slavery, and the male "right-to-rule" lives on today in less obvious ways. And women continue to satisfy their insatiable need for connection in destructive ways. I believe that Jesus came into the world to demonstrate that that kind of coping is inadequate and that we should, as Paul suggested, be united in the love, humility, contentment, and compassion of Christ (Phil 2:1–5). The needs of both men and women are best served in a community in which differences are recognized but not magnified, acknowledged but not exploited.

LISTENING AND LEARNING

I began work on this book with the hope of learning something from the Trinity that would teach men and women how to relate to one another in a more Christlike manner. In some respects that hope has been realized. But not in exactly the way I had expected. I expected an academic research and analysis exercise with a this-is-the-way-it-is conclusion. What I didn't expect was what hit me so compellingly in Sumner's *Men and Women in the Church*—the ability to *see* Paul's powerful head and body metaphor with its implications of interdependency. Like so many other people, I had read into biblical passages about God being the head of Christ and man being the head of woman, the idea of "headship." In doing so I had lost sight of the way Paul was illustrating interdependency within the Godhead and between men and women. The head and body metaphor Paul uses so frequently is now a vivid image for me. Now when I read passages such as 1 Corinthians 11 and Ephesians 5, I imagine a head with no body or a body with no head, and I am able to see what Paul is saying about relationship and interdependency in a way that I had not done before.

Also, I was deeply struck by Groothuis's observation that even if we were to read authority and headship into the passage in 1 Corinthians 11, the analogy of God as the head of Christ, and man as the head of woman, it would fail as a model supporting the subordination of women. Groothuis points out that the will of the Father and the Son is the same. There is no submission in a relationship in which the wills of the two people are perfectly aligned. For instance, if I want to go out for Mexican food and my husband wants to go out for Chinese, he could choose to submit to my wishes and go for Mexican. However, if we both want to go out for Mexican food it is nonsense to suggest that he is submitting if we go for Mexican. That is not submission, it is agreement.

And so, I would concur with Groothuis that even if it could be demonstrated that the Son is eternally subordinate to the Father, their relationship would not provide a meaningful analogy for the permanent subordination of women. The oneness of will and unity of being within the Godhead preclude such a comparison. That is not to say, however, that when Paul talks about God as the head of Christ and man as the head of woman, he is not trying to say *something*. I believe he is saying that we have a wondrously interdependent relationship and that honor, respect, acceptance, teamwork, and productivity should hold sway rather than discrimination, rejection, and limitations.

For me this book has been a personal journey, an opportunity for me to explore in depth some of the questions I have had regarding what it means to be a woman. As I look back over my life I have asked what God has been trying to teach me that he would like me to pass on to others. So I have listened to my life. I listened to the little grade school girl puzzling how *he* could mean *she*. I listened to the young housewife struggling to understand how permanent functional subordination could mean equality. I listened to the frustrated student confounded that both egalitarians and complementarians could claim to represent the historical orthodox view of the Trinity.

I offer this book as a witness to my personal journey and to my research regarding what it means to be equal. I trust that other men and women will be encouraged to listen to their own lives, to listen to what God is trying to teach us today, and to listen to what the Bible says about submission, authority, and interdependency.

Bibliography

Ambrose. *Hexameron, Paradise, and Cain and Abel.* In *The Fathers of the Church. Volume* 42. Translated by John J. Savage. New York: Fathers of the Church, 1961.

Aquinas, Thomas. *Basic Writings of Saint Thomas Aquinas,* edited by Anton C. Pegis. Volume 1. New York: Random House, 1944.

———. *Treatise on the Conservation and Government of Creatures.* In *Summa Theologica.* Translated by Fathers of the English Dominican Province. Benzinger Bros., 1947. http://www.ccel.org/ccel/Aquinas/summa.FP_Q108_A1.html July 7, 2007.

Athanasius. *Against the Arians.* NPNF2–04. *Athanasius: Select Works and Letters*|Christian Classics Ethereal Library. Discourse III.11 http://www.ccel.org/ccel/schaff/npnf204.xxxi.ii.iv.iii.html November 10, 2007.

———. *On the Incarnation.* Crestwood, NY: St. Vladimir's Seminary Press, 1980.

Augustine. *On the Trinity.* In *The Fathers of the Church.* Volume 45. Translated by Stephen McKenna. Washington DC: The Catholic University of America Press.

———. *On the Trinity.* I. http://www.newadvent.org/fathers/130101.htm July 3, 2007.

———. *On the Trinity.* II. http://www.newadvent.org/fathers/130102.htm June 27, 2007.

———. *On the Trinity.* IV. http://www.newadvent.org/fathers/130104.htm June 28, 2007

Barnes, Albert. *Notes on the New Testament: Corinthians.* Grand Rapids: Baker, 1962.

Barth, Karl. *Church Dogmatics,* edited by G. W. Bromiley and T. F. Torrance. Volume 1. Translated by G.W. Bromiley. Edinburgh: T & T Clark, 1975.

Basil. *On the Spirit.* Crestwood, New York: St. Vladimir's Seminary Press, 1980.

Belgic Confession. http://www.reformed.org/documents/BelgicConfession.html November 10, 2007.

Bettenson, Henry. *Documents of the Christian Church,* edited by Henry Bettenson. New York: Oxford University Press, 1981.

Bibliography

Bilezikian, Gilbert. *Beyond Sex Roles*. Second Edition. Grand Rapids: Baker, 2001.

Borland, James A. "Women in the Life and Teachings of Jesus." In *Recovering Biblical Manhood and Womanhood*, edited by John Piper and Wayne Grudem. Wheaton, IL: Crossway, 1991.

Calvin, John. *Commentary on the Epistles of Paul the Apostle to the Corinthians*. Volume 1. Translated by John Pringle. Grand Rapids: Eerdmans, 1948.

———. *Commentaries on the Epistles of Timothy, Titus, and Philemon*. Translated by Rev. William Pringle. Grand Rapids: Eerdmans, 1948

———. *Institutes*. Translated by Henry Beveridge, esq. Oak Harbor, WA: Logos Research Systems, 1997.

Carson, D. A. "Silent in the Churches." In *Recovering Biblical Manhood and Womanhood*. Edited by John Piper and Wayne Grudem. Wheaton, IL: Crossway, 1991.

Catholic Encyclopedia. S.V. "Saint John Damascene." *http://www.newadvent.org/cathen/08459b.htm December 7 2007*.

Chrysostom, John. "Homily XX on Ephesians." http://www.fisheaters.com/homilyxx.html November 25, 2007.

———. "Homily XXXI on the Epistle to the Romans." In *The Nicene and Post Nicene Fathers*. Volume XI. Grand Rapids: Eerdmans, 1997.

———. *On the Priesthood*. Crestwood, New York: St. Vladimir's Seminary Press, 1964.

Cladis, George. *Leading the Team-Based Church*. San Francisco: Jossey-Bass, 1999.

Creegan, Nicola Hoggard, and Christine D. Pohl. *Living on the Boundaries*. Downers Grove, IL: InterVarsity, 2005.

Dawn, Marva. *Powers, Weakness, and the Tabernacling of God*. Grand Rapids: Eerdmans, 2001.

Dictionary.com.Unabridged. V.1.1. http://dictionary.reference.com/browse/headship June 26, 2007.

Dunnam, Maxie D. *The Communicator's Commentary: Galatians, Ephesians, Philippians, Colossians, Philemon*, edited by Lloyd J. Ogilvie. Waco: Word, 1984.

Elliot, Elisabeth. "The Essence of Femininity." In *Recovering Biblical Manhood and Womanhood*, edited by John Piper and Wayne Grudem. Wheaton, IL: Crossway, 1991.

Enns, P. P. *The Moody Handbook of Theology*. Chicago: Moody, 1997.

Enns, Peter. *Inspiration and Incarnation*. Grand Rapids: Baker Academic, 2005.

Erickson, Millard J. *God in Three Persons*. Grand Rapids: Baker, 1995.

Fairbairn, Patrick. *Commentary on the Pastoral Epistles*. Grand Rapids: Zondervan, 1956.

Furlong, Monica. *Visions and Longings*. Boston: Shambhala, 1997.

Giles, Kevin. *Jesus and the Father*. Grand Rapids: Zondervan, 2006.

———. *The Trinity and Subordinationism*. Downers Grove, IL: InterVarsity, 2002.

Gonzalez, Justo L. *A History of Christian Thought*. Volume 3. Nashville: Abingdon, 1975.

Grenz, Stanley J., and Denise Muir Kjesbo. *Women in the Church*. Downers Grove, IL: InterVarsity Press, 1995.

Groothuis, Rebecca M. "Equal in Being, Unequal in Role." In *Discovering Biblical Equality*, edited by Ronald W. Pierce and Rebecca Merrill Groothuis. Downers Grove, IL: InterVarsity, 2004.

Grudem, Wayne. *Evangelical Feminism and Biblical Truth*. Sisters, Oregon: Multnomah, 2004.

———. "The Meaning of Kephale." In *Recovering Biblical Manhood and Womanhood*, edited by John Piper and Wayne Grudem. Wheaton, IL: Crossway, 1991.

———. *Systematic Theology*. Grand Rapids: Zondervan, 1994.

Henry, Carl F. H. *God, Revelation and Authority*. Volume 5. Waco: Word, 1982.

Henry, Matthew. *Matthew Henry's Commentary*. Volume 6. New York: Revell, n.d.

Hildegard of Bingen. *Scivias*. Translated by Mother Columba Hart and Jane Bishop. New York: Paulist, 1990.

Hodge, Charles. *An Exposition of the First Epistle to the Corinthians*. Philadelphia: Presbyterian Board of Publication, 1857.

House, H. Wayne. *The Role of Women in Ministry Today*. Nashville: Thomas Nelson, 1990.

Hull, Gretchen Gaebelein. *Equal to Serve*. Old Tappan, NJ: Revell, 1987.

John of Damascus. "Concerning the Holy Trinity." In *An Exact Exposition of the Orthodox Faith*. Book 1, Chap. VIII. http://www.ccel.org/ccel/schaff/npnf209.iii.iv.i.viii.html?highlight=john,37 December 7, 2007.

Keener, Craig S. *The IVP Bible Background Commentary, New Testament*. Downers Grove, IL: InterVarsity, 1993

Kimball, Cynthia Neal. "Nature, Culture and Gender Complementarity." In *Discovering Biblical Equality*, edited by Ronald W. Pierce and Rebecca Merrill Groothuis. Downers Grove, IL: InterVarsity, 2004.

Knight, George W., III. "Husbands and Wives as Analogues of Christ and the Church." In *Recovering Biblical Manhood and Womanhood*, edited by John Piper and Wayne Grudem. Wheaton, IL: Crossway, 1991.

————. *The New Testament Teaching on the Role Relationship of Men and Women*. Grand Rapids: Baker, 1977.

Liddon, Henry P. *Explanatory Analysis of St. Paul's First Epistle to Timothy*. New York: Longmans, Green and Co., 1897.

Luther, Martin. *Concerning the Ministry*. In *Luther's Works*, Vols. 32, 36, and 40. Philadelphia: Fortress, 1958.

McGrath, Alister E. *Studies in Doctrine*. Grand Rapids: Zondervan, 1997.

Moo, Douglas. "What Does It Mean Not to Teach or Have Authority Over Men." In *Recovering Biblical Manhood and Womanhood*, edited by John Piper and Wayne Grudem. Wheaton, IL: Crossway, 1991.

Newman, Barbara J. "Introduction to *Scivias* by Hildegard of Bingen." New York: Paulist, 1990.

Ortlund, Raymond C., Jr. "Male-Female Equality and Male Headship." In *Recovering Biblical Manhood and Womanhood*, edited by John Piper and Wayne Grudem. Wheaton, IL: Crossway, 1991.

Phelan, John E., Jr. *All God's People*. Chicago: Covenant, 2005.

Piper, John. "A Vision of Biblical Complementarity." In *Recovering Biblical Manhood and Womanhood*, edited by John Piper and Wayne Grudem. Wheaton, IL: Crossway, 1991.

Piper, John, and Wayne Grudem, "An Overview of Central Concerns." In *Recovering Biblical Manhood and Womanhood*, edited by John Piper and Wayne Grudem. Wheaton, IL: Crossway, 1991.

Purkiser, W. T. "The Holy Spirit." In *Exploring Our Christian Faith*, edited by W. T. Purkiser. Kansas City: Beacon Hill, 1978.

Rahner, Karl. *The Trinity*. Translated by Joseph Donceel. New York: Seabury, 1974.

Scanzoni, Letha, and Nancy Hardesty. *All We're Meant to Be*. Waco: Word, 1974.

Schreiner, Thomas R. "Head Coverings, Prophecies and the Trinity." In *Recovering Biblical Manhood and Womanhood*, edited by John Piper and Wayne Grudem. Wheaton, IL: Crossway, 1991.

Strauss, Mark L. *Distorting Scripture?* Downers Grove, IL: InterVarsity, 1998

Strong, A. H. *Systematic Theology*. Westwood, NJ: Revell (1907), 1967.

Sumner, Sarah. *Men and Women in the Church*. Downers Grove, IL: InterVarsity, 2003.

Torjesen, Karen Jo. *When Women Were Priests*. San Francisco: HarperSanFrancisco, 1995.

Tucker, Ruth A., and Walter Liefeld. *Daughters of the Church*. Grand Rapids: Zondervan, 1987.

Van Leeuwen, Mary Stewart. *Gender and Grace*. Downers Grove, IL: InterVarsity, 1990.

Walvoord, J. F., R. B. Zuck, and Dallas Theological Seminary. *The Bible Knowledge Commentary: An Exposition of the Scriptures*. Wheaton, IL: Victor, 1983–c1985.

Ware, Bruce A. "Equal in Essence, Distinct in Roles: Eternal Functional Authority and Submission Among the Essentially Equal Divine Persons of the Godhead." Paper presented at the 58th Annual Meetings, Evangelical Theological Society. Washington DC, November 16, 2006.

———. *Father, Son, and Holy Spirit*. Wheaton, IL: Crossway, 2005.

Warfield, Benjamin B. *The Person and Work of Christ*. Philadelphia: The Presbyterian and Reformed, 1970.

Webster's New World College Dictionary, edited by Michael Agnes. Fourth Edition. New York: Macmillan, 1999.

Weinrich, William. "Women in the History of the Church." In *Recovering Biblical Manhood and Womanhood*, edited by John Piper and Wayne Grudem. Wheaton, IL: Crossway, 1991.

Wiersbe, Warren. *The Biblical Expository Commentary*. Wheaton, IL: Victory, 1989. Electronic Edition, Scripture Press, 1996.